Blue Heaven

THE NEW YORK GIANTS INCREDIBLE RUN TO THE NFL CHAMPIONSHIP

FOREWORD

By Jerry Izenberg

THIS WAS A SEASON THAT will know no calendar. In the hearts and souls of that passionate congregation that gathers year after year in fair or foul weather to chase a dream within the concrete walls of the Giants' 100-yard cathedral, this was one that will remain evergreen.

In the years to come when they think of them, the power and grace of an Eli Manning throw will never fade ... Justin Tuck and Jason Pierre-Paul will forever be unmovable objects standing up to the teeth of an offense in Jets or Eagles or Cowboys jerseys ... and Victor Cruz, Hakeem Nicks and Mario Manningham will always catch the uncatchable passes.

When we recall this team and this season, our waistlines will seem to shrink and the gray will be gone from our hair. Because the lesson Tom Coughlin, the Giants' coach, taught us was simple but accurate:

"Hope may be a gossamer web but hope tested and justified through trial by emotional fire will morph into pure Teflon."

Consider the ugliest face of the 2011-2012 season.

The Giants were staggering toward a meltdown. Suddenly everything was wrong ... rallies fell short ... the defense became a leaky sieve on critical third downs ... the coach openly challenged their desire. The season that had begun with so much hope turned colder and crueler than the killer winds of the Meadowlands.

They lost four straight — the 49ers, the Eagles, the Saints and the Packers. Except for the Saints, they were games they could have and should have won.

Almost obscured by this fall from grace was Couglin's bed rock belief that this was a team with character. He harnessed that quality and turned the season into a magnificent tidal wave of redemption. He convinced them that it didn't matter who caught the pass or who made the sack or who threw the block. What mattered was that it was done.

It began with a rout of the Jets. They whipped the Eagles and the Cowboys and stormed into the playoffs. Atlanta posed no problem. Character? How about going into the frozen northland a seven-point underdog and beating the Packers in the Wisconsin cold. They went to San Francisco, underdogs again, and their beer-and-a-shot blue collar philosophy prevailed in the land of chardonnay and quiche.

And then, of course, the Super Bowl victory over the Pats. It's all here ... Eli's MVP performance ... Kenny Phillips kangarooing high above two receivers and batting away the touchdown pass that wasn't.., Ahmad Bradshaw and the winning score ... Justin Tuck charging forward and forcing Tom Brady into a safety ... and ... well ... well, don't listen to me. Hurry up and turn the page.

This season for the ages is all here.

CONTENTS

THE FIRST HALF

LEFT: The Giants' Tyler Sash and Victor Cruz run onto the field as time expires giving the Giants the win in the Super Bowl.
PHOTO BY TIM FARRELL

THE FIRST HALF

By Mike Garafolo

IN AN EFFORT TO DISCOVER who the 2011 Giants were, trace the arc of the first half of the season.

They were brilliant. They were underwhelming. They were struggling to put away a winless team. They were feeling like Super Bowl contenders. And while it was hard to determine what the truth was, it was seldom found anywhere in between the extremes of the opening eight games.

Perhaps those wild inconsistencies should have been expected. Training camp had been truncated by a lockout, which had lingered all summer and left Eli Manning and his receivers to a pickup brand of football at Hoboken High School. A compressed free-agency period was not particularly kind — or so it seemed at the time — to the Giants. They parted with several key veterans (Shaun O'Hara and Rich Seubert) and watched Steve Smith and Kevin Boss walk away, and a standoff between the front office and the star defensive end festered.

Whatever the explanation, the Giants' 6-2 start was anything but ordinary.

It started on the 10th anniversary of 9/11, with the Giants in Landover, Md. The start of a new season. The emotion associated with being one of the organizations most affected by the terrorist attacks. None of that seemed to resonate for the Giants in a debacle of a 28-14 loss — and they had plenty of reason to question themselves after Week 1.

"It's going to take this football team focusing a lot more than we did, putting on a better effort, a superior effort and we've got to have more purpose," Giants defensive tackle Chris Canty said that day. "We've got to have more purpose when we show up on gameday."

They weren't much more pleased a week later when they beat the Rams, 28-16, before the first glimpse of what these Giants could be was revealed.

A quick start in Philadelphia snowballed against the Eagles — and that was the afternoon Victor Cruz became a star. He broke two tackles on his way to a 74-yard touchdown in the first half, and then outleaped Nnamdi Asomugha, the presumed prize of the free-agent class, for another score as the Giants maximized their efforts all over the field.

"We definitely shut 'em up," running back Brandon Jacobs said. "There's no question about that."

A dramatic comeback at the Cardinals followed, with Eli Manning connecting with Cruz and Hakeem Nicks to deliver yet another amazing comeback in the desert — in the same building they had won Super Bowl XLII.

And just as the season was building, a phantom whistle and an old problem halted it. At home against the Seahawks, the Giants defense basically stood still as Doug Baldwin ran down the field, caught a pass and strolled in for the go-ahead touchdown. They

claimed they heard a whistle, but none of the officials stopped play. Manning marched his team toward a second consecutive come-from-behind win, but a pass near the goal line ricocheted off Cruz's hand and became an interception return for a touchdown.

"Poor performance, that's my fault," Coughlin said at the time, though he didn't sound very convinced of his own words. He later added: "It's always the head coach's fault. We didn't play well enough to win."

Even a pair of three-point victories at home against the Dolphins (20-17) and Bills (27-24) didn't do much to convince even the most faithful of fans that the Giants were ready to do much in November and December.

A trip to Foxborough, Mass., changed the lukewarm feelings of the fan base — and emboldened the Giants' team leaders.

Manning again got the better of Tom Brady, driving the Giants down the field and throwing the game-winning touchdown with 15 seconds left.

They looked ahead from that game and didn't see the same sort of second-half swoon that had become almost commonplace. In fact, they saw something much greater.

"We have great coaching, great players," defensive end Osi Umenyiora said, "and there's going to be no collapse here."

Said safety Antrel Rolle: "It's a remarkable feeling. This team's outstanding." ∎

Week 1: Stumbling Out of the Gate

REDSKINS 28, GIANTS 14

FedEx Field

Landover, Md.

It was one game, the first game, and one of 16 the Giants will play this year.

But don't try telling that to Chris Canty — not after a 28-14 loss to the Redskins.

"It's unacceptable in every regard," the Giants defensive tackle said. "... It's embarrassing."

It's not good, is what it is.

Not for a team that was shredded on the injury report and in free agency the past few months, with general manager Jerry Reese insisting his "plan" was still intact and that this was a competitive team.

Two minutes into the third quarter, rookie linebacker Ryan Kerrigan changed the complexion of the game. He avoided a cut block by Kareem McKenzie, tipped a pass from Eli Manning, picked it off and ran it back 9 yards for what proved to be the winning touchdown.

Of course, to boil this game down to Kerrigan's interception would be far too simplistic. There was a blocked field-goal attempt that could have cut Washington's lead to four points with about 11 minutes to play; an unnecessary-roughness penalty on Antrel Rolle when he merely had to touch tight end Fred Davis; and the failure to pick up a third-and-1 and a fourth-and-1 on runs by Ahmad Bradshaw.

Cue an agitated Canty.

"We just made the mistakes that Coach Coughlin continues to tell us that we can't make," said Canty, who had a sack and helped the defensive line keep the Redskins to only 2.8 yards per carry. "At some point, we as a team have got to listen."

— *Mike Garafolo*

ABOVE: Actor Robert DeNiro delivers a September 11 message on the JumboTron before the opening kickoff as the Giants open the 2011 season against the Redskins at FedEx Field. PHOTO BY ANDREW MILLS

RIGHT: Giants defensive end Justin Tuck gives fans a half-hearted thumbs up as he did not dress for the season's opener. PHOTO BY ANDREW MILLS

PREVIOUS: Giants quarterback Eli Manning is sacked by Redskins nose tackle Chris Neild in the third quarter. PHOTO BY ANDREW MILLS

LEFT: Giants wide receiver Hakeem Nicks dives for the pylon but was ruled down on the 1-yard line after a 68-yard catch in the first quarter. PHOTO BY ANDREW MILLS

BELOW: Redskins wide receiver Anthony Armstrong beats Giants defensive back Antrel Rolle and makes a key third-down catch near the goal line that set up a Redskins touchdown in the first half. PHOTO BY ANDREW MILLS

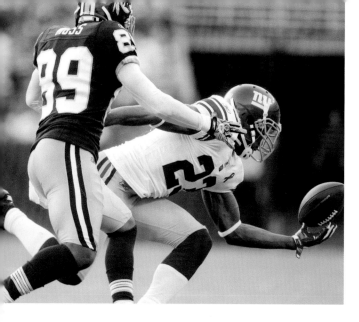

ABOVE: Giants defensive back Corey Webster almost makes a nifty one-hand interception on a pass intended for Redskins wide receiver Santana Moss in the fourth quarter. PHOTO BY ANDREW MILLS

RIGHT: Giants head coach Tom Coughlin questions head linesman Julian Mapp in the second half. PHOTO BY ANDREW MILLS

BELOW: Giants quarterback Eli Manning is dropped by Redskins linebacker Rocky McIntosh on the Giants second-to-last drive in the fourth quarter. PHOTO BY ANDREW MILLS

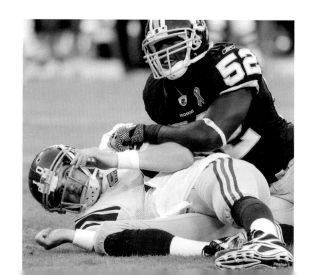

ABOVE: Redskins wide receiver Jabar Gaffney hauls in the back-breaking touchdown pass with Giants defensive back Corey Webster on the coverage in the fourth quarter. PHOTO BY ANDREW MILLS

Week 2: A Better Result, But Still Room to Grow

GIANTS 28, RAMS 16

MetLife Stadium
East Rutherford, N.J.

More offensive miscues. More coverage gaffes. More injuries.

But for at least one day, more points.

And with the way things are going for the Giants, they'll take it — with the expected caveat from their coach.

"Obviously, there's much to be improved upon, which is okay," Tom Coughlin said. "We'll accept that fact."

Only after a win, of course. Being 1-1 headed into a showdown with the Eagles, who have an identical record, the Giants were plenty happy last night.

But today and tomorrow, as they ready themselves for the self-proclaimed "Dream Team," they'll see on film how Eli Manning looked dreadful early, how the offense refused to grab momentum and how the defense allowed Sam Bradford to throw for a career-high 331 yards, albeit on a night he completed only 22 of 46 passes.

They'll see how some of the Giants' big plays were near-disasters with juggling catches that didn't have to be and resulted in injuries. Heck, they'll see even the celebrations were ugly and dangerous, with Michael Boley punctuating his 65-yard fumble return for a touchdown by firing the football into the face of poor Giants video-production intern Ryan Brown.

Brown, a YouTube sensation within minutes, said he was "getting blown up on Facebook" by his friends.

"That's good," Boley said, laughing once he was told Brown was fine. "Get him some pub."

But they'll also see that, after a season-opening pratfall, they figured out again how to win.

"Last week was almost like a wake-up call," David Diehl said. "Nobody wants to start the season that way. ... It's a positive direction we're moving in."

— *Mike Garafolo*

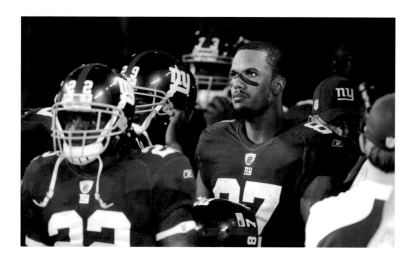

ABOVE: Domenik Hixon watches as the Giants host the St. Louis Rams at MetLife Stadium in East Rutherford. PHOTO BY ANDREW MILLS

RIGHT: Rams quarterback Sam Bradford barely gets the ball away as he is hit by Giants' defensive end Jason Pierre-Paul late in the first half. PHOTO BY ANDREW MILLS

OPPOSITE: The Giants' Hakeem Nicks catches a pass for a touchdown in the first half. PHOTO BY TIM FARRELL

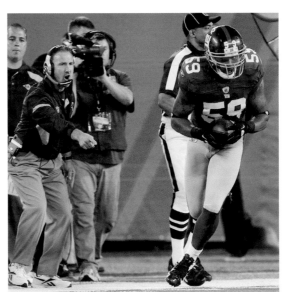

ABOVE: Giants running back Brandon Jacobs on a short yardage attempt in the first half. PHOTO BY ANDREW MILLS

LEFT: Rams head coach Steve Spagnuolo (left) points as Giants outside linebacker Michael Boley picks up a fumble and returns it for a touchdown in the first half. Spagnulo is the Giants' former defensive coordinator. PHOTO BY ANDREW MILLS

FAR LEFT: Giants defensive tackle Chris Canty bats down a pass by Rams quarterback Sam Bradford in the first half. PHOTO BY ANDREW MILLS

LEFT: The Giants' Domenik Hixon about to make a catch for a touchdown in the first half. PHOTO BY TIM FARRELL

BOTTOM LEFT: Quarterback Phil Simms (center) and the rest of the 1986 Super Bowl champion Giants are honored at halftime. PHOTO BY ANDREW MILLS

OPPOSITE: The Giants' Brandon Jacobs scores a touchdown in the second half. PHOTO BY TIM FARRELL

17

Week 3: A Dreamy Victory
GIANTS 29, EAGLES 16
Lincoln Financial Field
Philadelphia

It was practically a party in the Giants coaches' postgame elevator, the yelps and smacks of repeated high-five, palm-on-palm contact echoing off the metal walls.

Downstairs, not a sound could be heard in the church-like tunnel where the Eagles' players came off the field and headed to their locker room — not even the click-clacking of their cleats.

And down the hall in the visiting locker room, the Giants were teeming with the bravado that only a stunning, cathartic victory against their chief rivals could have produced.

Safeties coach David Merritt yelled, "Messed up the bookies in Vegas!" Brandon Jacobs boasted the Eagles' self-proclaimed "Dream Team" should "keep dreaming." Mathias Kiwanuka, asked to put what just happened in perspective, looked at the three reporters in front of him and said, "Did you pick us to win? Did you pick us to win? Did you pick us to win?"

Even the kicker, standing alongside the punter who tweeted the night before that this city was a "dump," was talking trash after the Giants ended their six-game losing streak to the Eagles.

This wasn't the typical Week 3 victory aftermath. It was, as Justin Tuck said, "a Super Bowl atmosphere."

For the first time since the lockout was lifted, a Giant said those words and nobody laughed.

The victory "really helped me believe even more in this football team," Tuck said. "… Now, there's no doubt whatsoever when we play our style of football, we can beat anybody."

— *Mike Garafolo*

ABOVE: Eagles quarterback Michael Vick is brought down on a hit by Giants free safety Antrel Rolle and fumbles the ball. The ball pops in the air and right into the hands of Eagles tackle Jason Peters during the Giants 29-16 victory over the Eagles at Lincoln Financial Field in Philadelphia. PHOTO BY ANDREW MILLS

LEFT: The Eagles' LeaSean McCoy is taken down by the Giants' Antrel Rolle and Jason Pierre-Paul in the fourth quarter. PHOTO BY TONY KURDZUK

OPPOSITE TOP: The Giants' Victor Cruz dances in the end zone after scoring the team's second touchdown in the first quarter. PHOTO BY TONY KURDZUK

OPPOSITE BOTTOM: Giants defensive end Jason Pierre-Paul cools himself off during a timeout as the Giants prepare to make a goal-line stand in the third quarter. PHOTO BY ANDREW MILLS

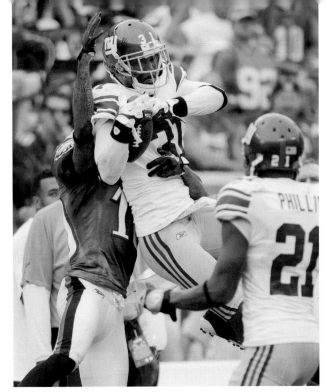

LEFT: The Giants' Aaron Ross makes an interception over the Eagles' DeSean Jackson in the fourth quarter. PHOTO BY TONY KURDZUK

FAR LEFT: Eagles linebacker Brian Rolle makes a defensive play on a long pass intended for Giants fullback Henry Hynoski in the end zone during the fourth quarter. PHOTO BY ANDREW MILLS

BELOW: Eagles cornerback Nnamdi Asomugha can't make the play as Giants wide receiver Victor Cruz regains control of the ball for a key 28-yard touchdown catch in the fourth quarter. PHOTO BY ANDREW MILLS

ABOVE: Giants running back Ahmad Bradshaw leaps past Eagles cornerback Nnamdi Asomugha and across the goal line late in the fourth quarter. PHOTO BY ANDREW MILLS

ABOVE: The Giants' Kenny Phillips (left) celebrates after making an interception of the Eagles' DeSean Jackson (right) during the Eagles' final drive, sealing the Giants' 29-16 victory. PHOTO BY TONY KURDZUK

LEFT: Eagles quarterback Michael Vick shows Giants quarterback Eli Manning his injured right hand after the game. PHOTO BY TONY KURDZUK

Week 4: Another Miracle in the Desert
GIANTS 31, CARDINALS 27

University of Phoenix Stadium
Glendale, Ariz.

It all looked remarkably familiar: the bewildered looks on the way to the locker room, the exhales, the relieved smiles, the what-the-heck-just-happened play to set up the winning touchdown in the left corner of the north end zone, the big sack on the final drive and the pass defended on the ball thrown to the opponent's best receiver.

This wasn't quite as important as their Super Bowl XLII win, but it sure seemed remarkably similar — and it has the Giants feeling their 3-0 record here is a sign wonders never cease inside this building that looks like a coiled snake.

"I could play in this building all 16 weeks," running back Brandon Jacobs said.

Three years, seven months and 28 days earlier, it was David Tyree's catch pressed against the side of his helmet. This time, it was Victor Cruz's dropping the ball at the end of a 19-yard catch — a move that could have been ruled a fumble.

But the officials determined Cruz had given himself up. By rule, that ended the play. Also by rule, it could not be challenged by the Cardinals.

One snap later, Eli Manning hit Hakeem Nicks for

a 29-yard touchdown past rookie cornerback Patrick Peterson for the game-winning score with 2:39 to play.

It was the second touchdown in 58 seconds for the Giants.

"These games are fun," Manning said. "I don't think you want to play in these every single week. ... Sometimes it's good to know you can do that, but we have to work on … not being down in the fourth quarter every time."

— Mike Garafolo

RIGHT: The Giants' linebacker Michael Boley reacts to dropping a ball that would have been an interception in the first half of the Giants game against the Seahawks at MetLife Stadium. PHOTO BY ARISTIDE ECONOMOPOULOS

OPPOSITE: The Giants' Hakeem Nicks scores a touchdown while being defended by the Seahawks' Walter Thurmond just before halftime. PHOTO BY ARISTIDE ECONOMOPOULOS

Week 5: Opportunity Lost — or Was it Blown?

SEAHAWKS 36, GIANTS 25

MetLife Stadium
East Rutherford, N.J.

Antrel Rolle "definitely" heard a whistle. Osi Umenyiora "thought" he did. And Mathias Kiwanuka noted "there was something."

Perhaps it was the screeching of the brakes being applied to the early-season optimism.

That was the feeling after a game that was decided by a 27-yard touchdown pass from backup quarterback Charlie Whitehurst to undrafted rookie Doug Baldwin against a confused defense and was iced by an interception by Eli Manning that bounced off Victor Cruz's hand for a 94-yard touchdown return by undrafted cornerback Brandon Browner.

And sealed by one other thing much less questionable than the phantom whistle.

"We played poorly. When you don't deserve to win, you don't win," coach Tom Coughlin said.

Or when you're allowing receivers to run free through the secondary.

That's what happened when Rolle and Aaron Ross got mixed up. Thinking the Seahawks were running a wide-receiver screen, Rolle passed the inside receiver (Baldwin) to Ross and focused on the outside receiver (Ben Obomanu). One problem: Ross did the same thing.

With safety Kenny Phillips favoring Sidney Rice on the other side of the field, Baldwin ran free. Whitehurst found Baldwin for the touchdown.

And the Giants were left to wonder what had happened.

"We have to take advantage when we have opportunities put in front of our face," Kiwanuka said. "We have a lot of individuals who went out and made spectacular plays. There were guys out there fighting. Now we just have to get everybody else on the field to do the same thing at the same time."

— *Mike Garafolo*

LEFT: The Giants' Victor Cruz, left, goes up for a ball against the Seahawks Kam Chancellor in the fourth quarter. The ball was tipped and Cruz was able to catch it with one hand and run it in for a touchdown.
PHOTO BY ARISTIDE ECONOMOPOULOS

OPPOSITE: Giants quarterback Eli Manning walks away from the line after the Giants were penalized for a delay of game call in the first quarter.
PHOTO BY ARISTIDE ECONOMOPOULOS

ABOVE: The Seahawks' Earl Thomas hits Giants kick returner Devin Thomas in the second half. PHOTO BY ARISTIDE ECONOMOPOULOS

ABOVE RIGHT: Giants running back D.J. Ware picks up some yardage in the second half. PHOTO BY ARISTIDE ECONOMOPOULOS

RIGHT: The Seahawks' Brandon Browner returns an interception for a touchdown in the fourth quarter. PHOTO BY ARISTIDE ECONOMOPOULOS

OPPOSITE: Seahawks strong safety Kam Chancellor falls as Giants wide receiver Victor Cruz makes the catch. PHOTO BY WILLIAM PERLMAN

Week 6: A "hard-earned win"

GIANTS 27, BILLS 24

MetLife Stadium
East Rutherford, N.J.

Had the Giants thought about what nearly was yesterday, perhaps it would have been.

How a good pass from Ryan Fitzpatrick could have been a touchdown to Stevie Johnson instead of an underthrown interception. How Leodis McKelvin's breaking on the ball on third-and-goal from the 5-yard line could have been a critical turnover and a potential defensive touchdown for the second straight week instead of a harmless incompletion. How another blown fourth-quarter lead could have been a disaster heading into the bye week and staring down the schedule that awaits.

But Corey Webster picked off Fitzpatrick's pass at the 4-yard line with 4:02 remaining, the Giants drove 76 yards to set up Lawrence Tynes' 23-yard, game-winning field goal with 92 seconds to play and the defense held on to head into the bye week with a victory.

"It tells me that guys are starting to trust and no one panicked," said defensive end Justin Tuck, who might have felt the drama more than most players because he was inactive and reduced to watching and cheering. "I've been on that sideline sometimes where everything seems like it's in disarray. Guys stepped up and played ball; that's what we need to do."

The Giants were close to disarray. Instead, they beat the Bills (4-2) to soften last week's upset loss to the Seahawks. They sit atop the NFC East. Tuck is talking about poise. And Tom Coughlin is looking at the upside.

Well, sort of.

"I'd like to be 6-0," he deadpanned. "But this is a hard-earned win."

— *Mike Garafolo*

ABOVE: Giants strong safety Kenny Phillips lines up for a play during the first half of the game between the Giants and the Bills at MetLife Stadium. PHOTO BY CHRIS FAYTOK

LEFT: Giants tight end Jake Ballard gains some ground during the second half against the Bills. PHOTO BY CHRIS FAYTOK

LEFT: Giants running back Ahmad Bradshaw leaps over Bills' Kelvin Sheppard, Nick Barnett and Marcell Dareus for his third rushing touchdown of the day during the third quarter. PHOTO BY CHRIS FAYTOK

BELOW: Giants defensive end Dave Tollefson gets to Bills quarterback Ryan Fitzpatrick. PHOTO BY WILLIAM PERLMAN

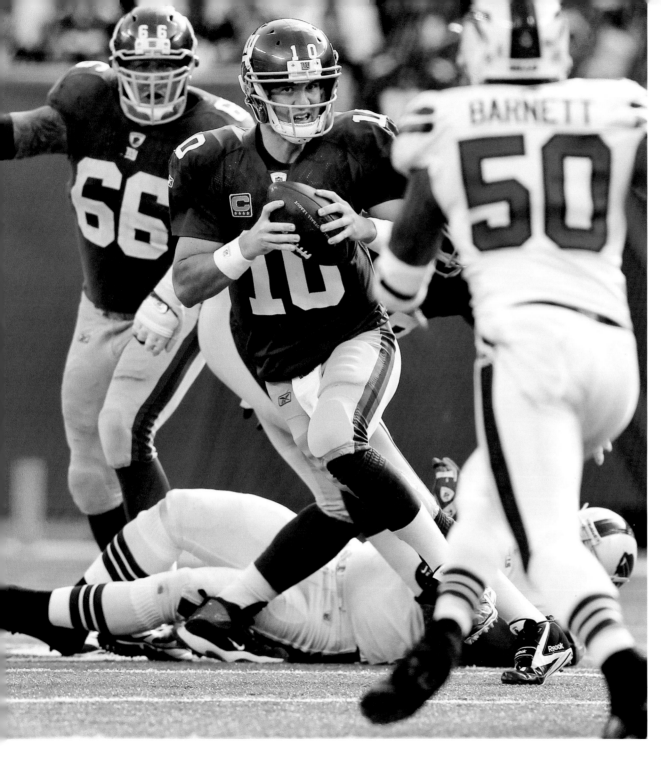

ABOVE: Giants cornerback Corey Webster intercepts a pass intended for Bills wide receiver Steve Johnson in the third quarter. PHOTO BY WILLIAM PERLMAN

LEFT: Giants quarterback Eli Manning scrambles as Bills inside linebacker Nick Barnett closes in during the second half. PHOTO BY CHRIS FAYTOK

OPPOSITE: Giants cornerback Corey Webster lets out a yell after intercepting a pass during the third quarter. PHOTO BY CHRIS FAYTOK

ABOVE: Quarterback Eli Manning and offensive coordinator Kevin Gilbride confer during the Giants' last drive. PHOTO BY ANDREW MILLS

LEFT: Giants running back Ahmad Bradshaw picks up three yards, dragging Bills defensive end Spencer Johnson in the fourth quarter. PHOTO BY ANDREW MILLS

ABOVE: Giants defensive end Osi Umenyiora jumps on the back of Giants defensive end Jason Pierre-Paul after Pierre-Paul batted down a Bills pass on fourth down late in the fourth quarter. PHOTO BY ANDREW MILLS

RIGHT: Fans hold up a sign as the Giants host the Bills at MetLife Stadium. PHOTO BY ANDREW MILLS

OPPOSITE: Victor Cruz can't shake off the Dolphins' Jimmy Wilson after a reception in the first half.
PHOTO BY TIM FARRELL

Week 8: Nearly Tripped Up

GIANTS 20, DOLPHINS 17

MetLife Stadium
East Rutherford, N.J.

Good teams should obliterate bad teams. That's the view from the outside, anywhere from the stands at MetLife Stadium to the Vegas Strip.

On the inside, it's how Tom Coughlin put it last week when talking about the Dolphins: "Respect all, fear none."

So the Giants' victory over winless Miami, which required a 25-yard touchdown pass from Eli Manning to Victor Cruz with 5:58 to play, might have looked like a disappointment from the outside and an indication this team is in trouble with arguably the toughest remaining schedule in the NFL to play.

But inside a locker room that was, by all indications, calm and businesslike at halftime, it was another strong finish, regardless of the opponent's record.

"Guys are not getting down on each other, guys aren't bickering, they just stay in the game and keep fighting," said Corey Webster, whose interception of Matt Moore sealed the game with 1:44 to play. "If we continue to do that, we can do something special here."

First of all, let's be clear about one thing: There was nothing "special" about this victory. And if the Giants keep allowing teams to run the ball while failing to do so themselves, continue to drop passes and don't play better in the first half, they're not headed for anything "special" or, well, Super. Not with the Patriots, 49ers, Saints, Packers, Eagles, Cowboys and Jets on their schedule.

And after needing to hang on against the Dolphins, they know that.

— *Mike Garafolo*

RIGHT: Giants running back Brandon Jacobs stretches during warm-ups. PHOTO BY WILLIAM PERLMAN

FAR RIGHT: Giants wide receiver Victor Cruz breaks away from Dolphins strong safety Yeremiah Bell for the winning touchdown. PHOTO BY WILLIAM PERLMAN

BELOW: The Giants' Eli Manning is pressured by the Dolphins' Karlos Dansby in the first half. PHOTO BY TIM FARRELL

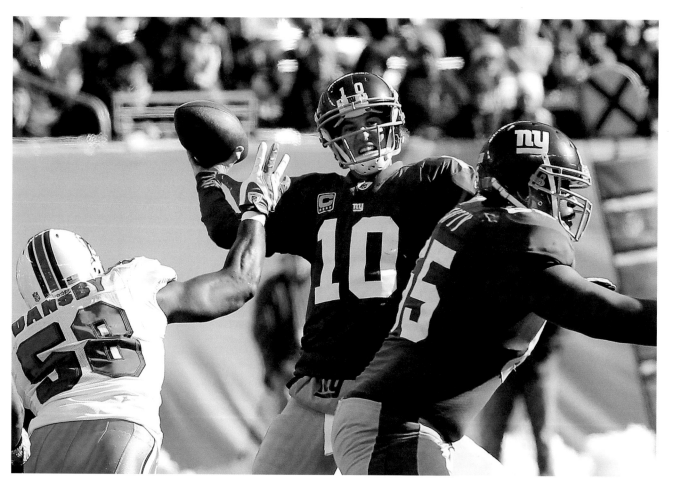

LEFT: Giants defensive end Osi Umenyiora sacks Dolphins quarterback Matt Moore in the fourth quarter.
PHOTO BY WILLIAM PERLMAN

OPPOSITE: Giants linebacker Jacquian Williams, center, gets to the Dolphins Reggie Bush on a fourth-quarter punt return, with the help of Justin Tryon, left, and Derrick Martin, right.
PHOTO BY WILLIAM PERLMAN

Week 9: Too Bold to Fold
GIANTS 24, PATRIOTS 20

Gillette Stadium
Foxborough, Mass.

Antrel Rolle didn't want the defense to "fold" in the face of this perceived mismatch with Tom Brady and the Patriots' passing game. Tom Coughlin didn't want Brandon Jacobs to buckle and drop him as he carried him in celebration. And Osi Umenyiora finished a question about this being the time of the season …

"We fold?" the defensive end said.

Well, yeah. But after Eli Manning bested Brady and the Patriots again, this time with a 1-yard touchdown pass to Jake Ballard with 15 seconds remaining, there was a reason to believe things might end differently this season.

The Giants don't plan on folding. Deal them in.

"Not this time, man. We've been through that too many times," said Umenyiora, part of a pass rush that once again harassed Brady. "We have great coaching, great players and there's going to be no collapse here."

Credit a lot of people for allowing such talk in that locker room: Coughlin and his staff for getting this injury-ravaged team ready; Manning for backing up the "elite" talk; Jacobs for correcting his attitude; Ballard for making a leaping, 28-yard catch on third-and-10 on the final drive; Victor Cruz for drawing a 20-yard pass-interference penalty to set up Ballard's touchdown.

Really, everybody in the white jerseys.

"It's a remarkable feeling, this team's outstanding. This is why I became a Giant — to play in games like this," Rolle said. "Everybody's crunked, everybody's swagged out, we went out there and we represented something."

— *Mike Garafolo*

ABOVE: Giants strong safety Kenny Phillips tackles Patriots wide receiver Wes Welker. PHOTO BY WILLIAM PERLMAN

RIGHT: Giants defensive ends Jason Pierre-Paul and Osi Umenyiora get to Patriots quarterback Tom Brady in the second quarter.
PHOTO BY WILLIAM PERLMAN

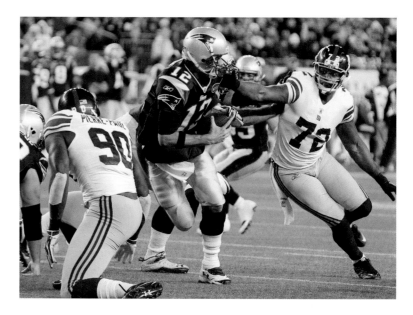

ABOVE: The Giants' Jake Ballard makes a catch in the second half against the Patriots at Gillete Stadium. PHOTO BY TIM FARRELL

ABOVE: Giants middle linebacker Jacquian Williams jumps up after a fumble recovery by Patriots quarterback Tom Brady.
PHOTO BY WILLIAM PERLMAN

RIGHT: Giants running back Brandon Jacobs scores in the third quarter. PHOTO BY WILLIAM PERLMAN

ABOVE: The Giants' Eli Manning calls signals in the second half. PHOTO BY TIM FARRELL

LEFT: Giants tight end Jake Ballard is tackled by Patriots outside linebacker Brandon Spikes. PHOTO BY WILLIAM PERLMAN

FAR LEFT: The Patriots' Aaron Hernandez drives in a touchdown after a catch in the second half. PHOTO BY TIM FARRELL

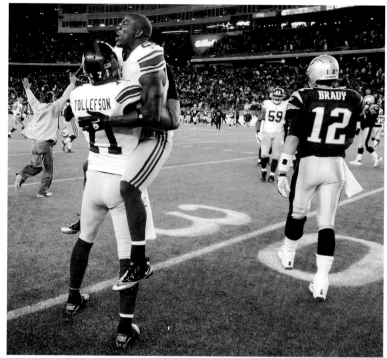

ABOVE: Giants defensive end Dave Tollefson and free safety Antrel Rolle celebrate the win as Patriots quarterback Tom Brady walks off the field. PHOTO BY WILLIAM PERLMAN

LEFT: Patriots cornerback Kyle Arrington is late as Giants wide receiver Mario Manningham makes a touchdown catch in the fourth quarter. PHOTO BY WILLIAM PERLMAN

OPPOSITE: Giants wide receivers Victor Cruz, left, and Mario Manningham celebrate Manningham's touchdown in the fourth quarter. PHOTO BY WILLIAM PERLMAN

THE COLLAPSE

By Mike Garafolo

PICK A MOMENT, AND THAT's when the season could have started to unravel.

Maybe it would have been the fourth-down play in San Francisco, where Eli Manning failed to deliver yet another comeback — and the doubts about how the Giants might be souring in their second-half schedule creeped in.

Or maybe during a fall-flat-on-their-face loss at home in primetime against the Eagles, when one loss became two.

Or it could have come at the hand of Drew Brees, he of the record-setting season and maestro of a passing attack for which the Giants still have no answers.

It even might have been revealed in a high-quality loss to the Packers, when, for all the good that came of a 38-35 setback against the only team still unbeaten at that point in the season, it was hard to ignore that four losses in a row had leveled the Giants' record at 6-6.

And what about an inexplicable loss at home

LEFT: Giants defensive end Justin Tuck sits dejected on the bench as the Giants fall to the Redskins, 23-10, on Dec. 18 at MetLife Stadium in East Rutherford, N.J.
PHOTO BY ANDREW MILLS

---

against the Redskins, with the stakes and scenarios surrounding a playoff berth so obvious?

Instead, the story of this Giants season is much better told as the tale of how none of that, in fact, crushed the will of this team.

They marched out of Candlestick Park — having been stymied, beaten up and turned away — full of confidence. They openly pined for another shot at the 49ers.

They responded to their worst performance of the season, when Brees directed the Saints offense to 577 yards, with yet another showcase of Eli Manning's elite abilities nearly outdid Aaron Rodgers'.

And the NFC East, ultimately the ticket to the postseason for the Giants, didn't slip from their grasps — at least not entirely. While the losses to the Eagles and Redskins were damning — the latter had teammates sniping at one another for sitting out practices with injuries that Antrel Rolle decided were "nicks and bruises."

Said the safety: "We've got to give ourselves better opportunities, man."

Whether the Giants would have been able to look at the exceptionally trying circumstances in this six-game stretch and still see a glass half-full had they not landed in the playoffs is something we'll never know.

That they eventually did reach the postseason, though, is largely a credit to the fingertips on Jason Pierre-Paul's left hand, which deflected a potential game-tying field goal and preserved a victory against

the Cowboys.

And Manning once again delivered in the clutch, throwing for 400 yards and a pair of touchdowns — and leading the Giants back from a 34-22 deficit in the fourth quarter. That performance, just the latest in an outstanding season for Manning, even impressed coach Tom Coughlin.

"Sometimes, I wish I was in that huddle," Coughlin said of Manning's late-game drives, "so I could hear what was being said."

Said team president John Mara: "It'd be nice to have an easy one, but I don't think that's in our DNA."

If nothing else was obvious as the final stretch approached, nothing would come easy for the 2011 Giants. ∎

LEFT: Giants outside linebacker Michael Boley prepares his team to take the field before opening kickoff. PHOTO BY ANDREW MILLS

OPPOSITE: Giants defensive end Jason Pierre-Paul during pregame warmups. PHOTO BY ANDREW MILLS

BELOW LEFT: Giants general manager Jerry Reese (left) and team owner John Mara during pregame warmups. PHOTO BY ANDREW MILLS

BELOW: Giants wide receiver Mario Manningham makes a diving catch in the first half. PHOTO BY ANDREW MILLS

play and a two-point conversion.

That spanned 70 seconds and turned a 13-12 Giants lead into a two-touchdown advantage for the Niners with 12:21 to play. The Giants pulled within a touchdown after Hakeem Nicks' 32-yard score but couldn't finish off their final drive.

"We had a chance, man," said D.J. Ware, who had 34 yards on nine carries. "We just didn't take advantage of it."

— *Mike Garafolo*

Week 10: Finally, the Giants Run Out of Time
49ERS 27, GIANTS 20

Candlestick Park
San Francisco

They had done it before — five times, in fact — so it's easy to see why they figured it was about to happen once more.

Despite giving up two touchdowns in just over a minute and losing a pair of key defensive players to injury, the Giants could see their way to their sixth fourth-quarter comeback of the year when they drove deep into 49ers territory.

But a team that had kept saying it couldn't continue to live dangerously proved why when its

final drive stalled at the Niners' 10-yard line when Patrick Willis wrapped up Jake Ballard and Justin Smith knocked down Eli Manning's pass with 34 seconds to play.

"You can call it percentages or whatever you want," coach Tom Coughlin said, "but we're prepared to excel in that area and we've done just that. I'm thinking we're going to win and so was everybody else."

Everybody but the 49ers, who took control of this game thanks to a sequence that included a 31-yard touchdown from Alex Smith to Vernon Davis against a confused, banged-up Giants defense, Carlos Rogers' second interception of Manning two plays later, Kendall Hunter's 17-yard touchdown run on the next

ABOVE: Giants defensive end Osi Umenyiora (center) sacks 49ers quarterback Alex Smith in the second half.
PHOTO BY ANDREW MILLS

ABOVE LEFT: Giants defensive end Justin Tuck has 49ers quarterback Alex Smith wrapped up, but Smith was able to get the ball away in the second quarter.
PHOTO BY ANDREW MILLS

OPPOSITE: Eli Manning watches as 49ers cornerbacks Carlos Rogers and Tarell Brown, right, celebrate Rogers' interception of a Manning pass late in the first half.
PHOTO BY ANDREW MILLS

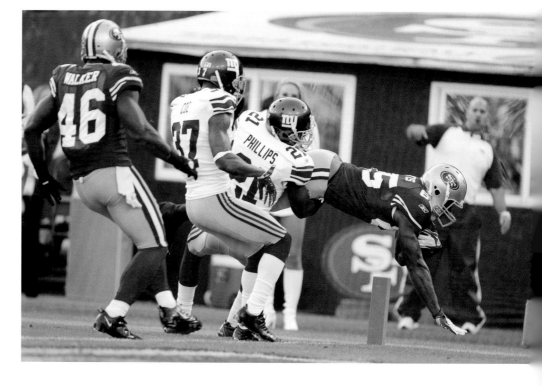

OPPOSITE AND ABOVE: 49ers tight end Vernon Davis leaps up and over Giants strong safety Kenny Phillips for a 31-yard touchdown catch in the fourth quarter. PHOTOS BY ANDREW MILLS

Week 11: Knocked From Their Perch
EAGLES 17, GIANTS 10

MetLife Stadium
East Rutherford, N.J.

Last year, it happened quickly: 28 points in seven minutes, with the final 14 seconds a nightmare flash of DeSean Jackson for the Giants.

This year, the final stages of the Eagles' victory were much more methodical: an 18-play, 80-yard drive over 8 minutes, 51 seconds that included six third-down conversions.

The last of the conversions was a dagger — an 8-yard pass from Vince Young to Riley Cooper in the back of the end zone for the winning touchdown with 2:45 to play.

The Giants' fate then dragged out over a failed comeback attempt that ended when Jason Babin hit Eli Manning. Derek Landri recovered the fumble to seal the game. And just that quickly — or slowly — the "Dream Team" isn't quite dead yet.

"As disappointed a feeling as we've had around here in a long time," Giants coach Tom Coughlin said. "I didn't like the way we played."

Coughlin used some other words, in addition to the ones Victor Cruz described as "choice" ones in the postgame locker room. They were: "pathetic" (to describe the Giants' 29 yards rushing), "outplayed" (his assessment of the offensive line's play) and "poor" (the overall performance).

Basically, Coughlin didn't like the way his players

responded to being hit in the mouth by a desperate team with its season on the line and featuring a backup quarterback in Young.

And given what lies ahead in the next two weeks (at the Saints, home against the Packers), this is anything but a runaway in the NFC.

And it might all be slipping away — quickly.

— *Mike Garafolo*

ABOVE: Giants defensive back Deon Grant watches as Eagles wide receiver Riley Cooper hauls in the game-winning touchdown late in the fourth quarter. PHOTO BY ANDREW MILLS

RIGHT: Eagles defensive end Derek Landri is there to pick up the loose ball as Eli Manning fumbles while being sacked by defensive end Jason Babin late in the fourth quarter. PHOTO BY ANDREW MILLS

OPPOSITE: Manning lies on the field after he fumbles the ball late in the second half. PHOTO BY TIM FARRELL

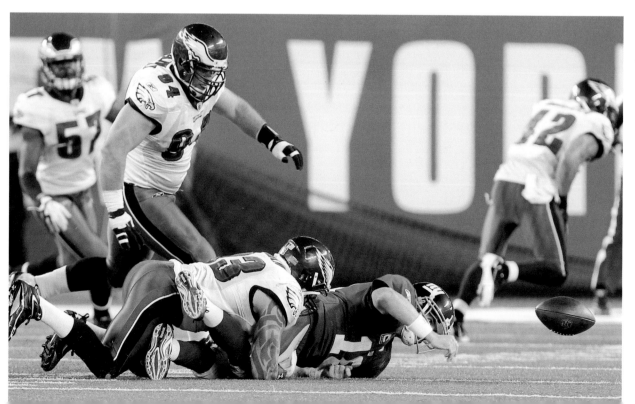

Week 12: Blown Away in the Big Easy

SAINTS 49, GIANTS 24

Superdome
New Orleans

The Giants claimed it would be different this time, that they'd come out fighting, that they'd swag the dog, or whatever Antrel Rolle vowed would occur, that they'd have "poise in the noise" and that they weren't in the middle of a second-half swoon.

Nope. No. Eh, hardly. Prove it.

Following an uplifting victory over the Patriots three weeks ago, the Giants have begun to melt down. Again.

Drew Brees threw all over them like it was 2009 in a game that was about as bad as it gets and knocked them a full game behind the Cowboys in the NFC East. Considering the Packers are on deck after a short week, how can it possibly get better quickly?

"That's not Giant football, what you saw tonight," defensive tackle Chris Canty said of the defense allowing 577 yards, the second-most in franchise history. "We've got to figure out a way to get back to that."

That was a theme coach Tom Coughlin echoed: the preparation was great, the energy was great and "we just didn't cover them."

That's stating the obvious.

Brees threw for 363 yards and four touchdowns (two each to Lance Moore and Jimmy Graham) — giving him eight in his past two games against the Giants — and even ran for one. Meanwhile, the Giants made repeated mistakes to kill any hopes of staying in this one: missed tackles, dropped passes, dropped interceptions, fumbles, missed sacks and blown coverages.

"We've got to determine where we want to be," Rolle said. "We're not going to throw the towel. … We're not that kind of team."

— Mike Garafolo

PACKERS 38, GIANTS 35

MetLife Stadium
East Rutherford, N.J.

There was a lot of optimism in the Giants' locker room, plenty of back slaps, atta boys, references to the 2008 close loss to the Patriots and talk of all the good things to take from this game.

And then, there was Dave Tollefson, sitting in the farthest corner of the room, elbows on his knees and speaking in a tone that suggested he had not just participated in a moral victory.

What Tollefson saw was a defense that allowed Green Bay to go 68 yards in 55 seconds to set up Mason Crosby's 31-yard winning field goal as time expired in the Packers' 38-35 victory that preserved their perfect season (12-0) and extended the tail-spinning Giants' losing streak to four games.

"Eli (Manning) and the offense do a great job, go down there and score to tie us up and we just — pffft," Tollefson said, opting for a razzing commentary rather than a breakdown of what happened. "Come on now, we're better than that."

We've got a couple of interesting debates on our hands: Are the Giants better than what they showed? And are they a team that can positively spin a loss at this point in the season?

"There's no solace in playing well and losing," Tom Coughlin said. "We're way past that. ... We'll battle, we'll battle. We have to find a way to win."

— *Mike Garafolo*

LEFT: Packers quarterback Aaron Rodgers runs away from Giants defensive end Jason Pierre-Paul during the first half. PHOTO BY JOHN O'BOYLE

FAR LEFT: Eli Manning is hit by Packers' Clay Matthews after getting off a second-half pass. PHOTO BY JOHN O'BOYLE

RIGHT: Packers' Jordy Nelson pulls in a pass as Giants' Will Blackmon chases.
PHOTO BY JOHN O'BOYLE

BELOW LEFT: The Giants' Justin Tuck sacks Aaron Rodgers in the first half.
PHOTO BY TIM FARRELL

BELOW RIGHT: Aaron Rodgers loses his helmet after a sack by Justin Tuck.
PHOTO BY WILLIAM PERLMAN

ABOVE: Hakeem Nicks scores a touchdown with 58 seconds left in the game, followed by a two-point conversion that tied the game, 35-35. PHOTO BY JOHN O'BOYLE

LEFT AND BELOW: Eli Manning and the fans are glum after the 38-35 loss to the Packers.
PHOTOS BY, LEFT, JOHN O'BOYLE AND, RIGHT, WILLIAM PERLMAN

FAR LEFT: The Packers' Mason Crosby kicks the winning field goal as time expires. PHOTO BY WILLIAM PERLMAN

Week 14: By the Tip of a Finger

GIANTS 37, COWBOYS 34

Cowboys Stadium
Arlington, Texas

Tom Coughlin didn't lie. He was mentally preparing himself for an extra period.

Little did Coughlin know the second icing of the Cowboys' kicking unit in as many weeks was about to help save the Giants' chaotic season. Dan Bailey's 47-yard field goal was good for only a moment. Coughlin's timeout before the snap had negated it.

The second attempt was blocked by Jason Pierre-Paul with 1 second remaining, allowing the Giants to move into a first-place tie in the NFC East.

"He got a finger on it," Coughlin said, "and that was enough."

Said Pierre-Paul: "I looked at the sideline and everybody was just going crazy, so I knew something had happened."

Yeah, the Giants' season had just been revived.

From a 6-2 start, the Giants had pushed their playoff hopes to the edge of the cliff the past four weeks. For much of the night against the Cowboys, they nudged it about as far as it could go. And then, they somehow brought it back.

Eli Manning threw an 8-yard touchdown to Jake Ballard and Brandon Jacobs scored from a yard out with 46 seconds to play to overcome a 12-point deficit in the final 5:41 — reinforcing that no matter how this season ends, the Giants won't make it easy.

"It'd be nice to have an easy one," said team president John Mara, who might not make it through the season with how involved he gets in games, "but I don't think that's in our DNA."

— *Mike Garafolo*

LEFT: Justin Tuck takes a knee as Giants cornerback Corey Webster catches a pass during pregame warmups.
PHOTO BY ANDREW MILLS

OPPOSITE: Giants defensive linemen, including Chris Canty, center, get fired up prior to the game against the Cowboys.
PHOTO BY ANDREW MILLS

LEFT: The referee signals a safety after Cowboys' quarterback Tony Romo, left, was sacked in the end zone by Jason Pierre-Paul. PHOTO BY ANDREW MILLS

FAR LEFT: Brandon Jacobs hurdles Cowboys safety Gerald Sensabaugh on his way to a big gain in the first quarter. PHOTO BY ANDREW MILLS

BELOW: Giants defensive back Deon Grant runs with the ball after he recovered a fumble by Cowboys running back Felix Jones late in the second quarter. PHOTO BY ANDREW MILLS

ABOVE: Tony Romo is sacked by Jason Pierre-Paul. PHOTO BY ANDREW MILLS

LEFT: Brandon Jacobs gets a hug from fellow running back Ahmad Bradshaw after second-quarter touchdown run. PHOTO BY ANDREW MILLS

OPPOSITE: Giants wide receiver Mario Manningham beats Cowboys cornerback Terence Newman to make a key fourth-down catch in the fourth quarter. PHOTO BY ANDREW MILLS

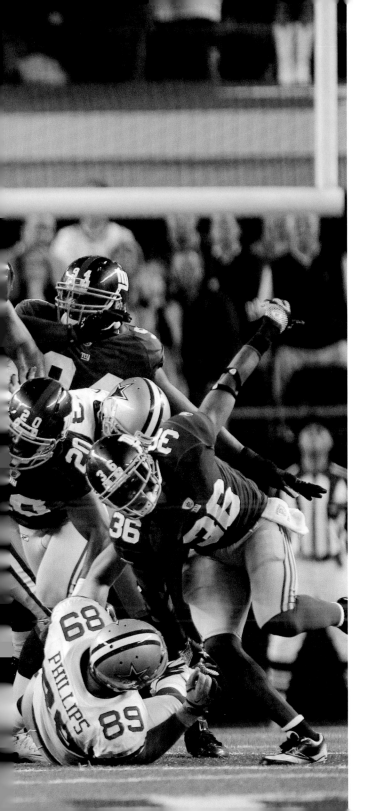

ABOVE: Eli Manning and lineman Chris Snee celebrate a touchdown. PHOTO BY ANDREW MILLS

LEFT: Giants' Jason Pierre-Paul blocks the game-tying field goal attempt by Cowboys kicker Dan Bailey at the end of the game. PHOTO BY ANDREW MILLS

Week 15: An urgent situation

REDSKINS 23, GIANTS 10

MetLife Stadium
East Rutherford, N.J.

Usually after a Giants loss, it's Tom Coughlin talking about how good or bad the previous week of practice was.

Yesterday, it was an eye-rolling Antrel Rolle who tried to explain the team's seemingly inexplicable loss to the Redskins by pointing to a week of preparation that just wasn't as sharp as it needed to be.

"It starts in practice, man. This (stuff) starts in practice," the Giants' outspoken safety said. "And you know what? We need to have everyone on the field. If you're injured, so be it, you're injured. We understand that.

"But nicks and bruises? Everyone needs to be on the field because we're not getting better like this."

No, they're getting worse, and so are their chances of making the playoffs.

The Giants need to make up a game on Dallas in the final two weeks to win the NFC East. The simplest scenario is to beat the Jets and Cowboys the next two weeks. Perhaps the urgency of the situation will rally the team.

Then again, they probably should've won yesterday against the Redskins, who have two wins over the Giants and only three against the rest of the league.

"Honestly, I'm standing up here and I'm babbling because I don't know how to answer your questions," defensive end Justin Tuck said. "I really don't know what to tell you."

Said Rolle: "We're 10 times better than what we showed out there on the field today. I don't know man, I don't know. I don't know."

— Mike Garafolo

LEFT: The Redskins' Oshiomogho Atogwe makes a diving interception on an Eli Manning pass that was deflected in the second quarter. PHOTO BY ANDREW MILLS

FAR LEFT: Giants' Kenny Phillips picks off a Rex Grossman pass intended for wide receiver Jabar Gaffney in the first quarter. PHOTO BY ANDREW MILLS

BELOW: Giants defensive end Jason Pierre-Paul was fined $10,000 for making this helmet-to-helmet contact with Redskins quarterback Rex Grossman in the first half. PHOTO BY ANDREW MILLS

LEFT: The Giants' Bear Pascoe leaps over the Redskins' Perry Riley and Josh Wilson in the second half. PHOTO BY TIM FARRELL

OPPOSITE: Eli Manning is hit while releasing the ball in the second quarter as Redskins' London Fletcher tries to bat the ball down. PHOTO BY ANDREW MILLS

BELOW: Redskins cornerback Josh Wilson picks off a pass intended for Giants wide receiver Mario Manningham. PHOTO BY ANDREW MILLS

RIGHT: Eli Manning walks past head coach Tom Coughlin after throwing a fourth-quarter interception in the end zone.
PHOTO BY ANDREW MILLS

FAR RIGHT: The ball comes loose as Eli Manning is sandwiched by Redskins Barry Cofield, top, and Ryan Kerrigan on a fourth-down play late in the game.
PHOTO BY ANDREW MILLS

PLAYING LIKE THEY MEAN IT

By Mike Garafolo

IT WAS A FITTING END to a week of chirping between the Giants and Jets. The two resident yappers on each side— Brandon Jacobs and Rex Ryan — nearly coming to blows at what's usually handshake and hug time.

"Time to shut up, fat boy!" Jacobs yelled.

At that point, Jacobs claims Ryan tried to come after him "the way his old man went after (Kevin) Gilbride." To which, in this season of yuletide cheer, he sent the merriest of holiday greetings.

"You're talking to the wrong Giant," Jacobs said he yelled, "because I will kick your (butt)!"

We knew it would end this way, with the winning team getting the final say after days, weeks, months and years of trash talk. After an oft-sloppy but always entertaining 29-14 victory, it was the Giants breaking from the "talk is cheap" part of Tom Coughlin's mantra after delivering on the "play the

game" portion to set up a showdown with the Dallas Cowboys for the NFC East title next Sunday.

Chris Canty's sack of Mark Sanchez in the end zone for a safety with 2:13 to play was pretty much the difference and set off celebrations that included Justin Tuck doing Fireman Ed's "J-E-T-S" chant with a drop kick at the end.

Time to shut up indeed.

Still, even in victory, a hobbled Coughlin declined to get into the back-and-forth jawing. But he did notice how it sparked his team.

Players who admitted they did nothing after getting "punched in the mouth" by the Eagles a few weeks ago, and had lost five of their last six, finally showed some fight.

"It was shocking," Coughlin said of the way his team came out in practice last week. "I looked up and said, 'Is that the same guys?' They had great purpose and the way they practiced is the way they played."

Hard. Fast. Aggressive.

That's how the Giants played. Okay, maybe not all day on offense. Eli Manning was only 9-for-27 and unable to exploit the "decent" Darrelle Revis, while the running game sputtered until late when Jacobs had a 28-yard run and Ahmad Bradshaw had a game-clinching 19-yard touchdown.

LEFT: Giants running back Brandon Jacobs breaks free for a 13-yard gain on a short pass as he's tackled by Jets defensive back Donald Strickland during the first half.
PHOTO BY CHRIS FAYTOK

But they played that way nearly all game on defense. Perry Fewell's unit allowed a season-low in points, recorded five sacks, picked off Sanchez twice and for once dictated the tempo, thanks to a simple scheme that stressed comfort level for their defensive backs over confusion for the offense.

"We had a game plan and he stuck with it 120 percent," safety Antrel Rolle said. "I just kept getting in his ear, telling him, 'Stay with the game plan. We're going to make it work for you.'

"(Sanchez) tried to throw the ball (59) times and not even 300 yards (259, to be exact), so that's definitely a win in our books."

With the drum softly being pounded by some for Fewell to be canned (and Steve Spagnuolo, who hasn't even been fired yet, to replace him), the Giants' defense made huge plays when it mattered.

Kenny Phillips opened the fourth quarter with an interception of a ball Sanchez threw over Jeremy Kerley's head. The Giants turned that into a field goal and a 20-7 lead.

On the next drive, Jason Pierre-Paul seemed to create another turnover by stripping Sanchez after extending his long arms to beat D'Brickashaw Ferguson for the second time on the day. A challenge by Ryan reversed the call.

"We're going to have to revisit the 'tuck rule,'" said Coughlin, who has been baffled by replay challenges in recent weeks. "Unbelievable."

The Giants got their turnover four plays later when Nick Mangold's snap never made it to Sanchez's hands for a fumble recovered by Jacquian Williams in the end zone.

After an ill-advised pass resulted in an interception by David Harris, the Giants seemingly had their third turnover of the quarter when Linval Joseph knocked the ball from Sanchez's hand. But again, a challenge by the Jets ended with a reversal because it was ruled Sanchez's arm was coming forward.

This time, Sanchez turned it into a touchdown on a 1-yard scramble after he ran for 11 yards.

With 7:17 to play, it was a 20-14 game. Given the way the Giants have responded to adversity this year, this smelled like trouble.

Except ...

"We were able to make more plays than they did at the end of the football game," Canty said, "and that was the difference."

None was bigger than Canty's sack, which came after Kerley fair caught a punt by Steve Weatherford at the 8-yard line with 2:13 to play. Canty heard Mangold's calls and realized he'd have a one-on-one matchup with guard Matt Slauson.

"I went speed-to-power to get to the edge," Canty said. "I was able to beat him and I was able to close on the quarterback when he still had the ball."

A recovery of an onside free kick and Bradshaw's touchdown kick-started the celebration.

Though Jacobs did get a head start in the fourth quarter by mocking the "J-E-T-S" chant after his long run.

"With crash landing at the end," he said with a chuckle. ■

ABOVE: Giants fullback Henry Hynoski gets ready for a first-half play. PHOTO BY CHRIS FAYTOK

LEFT ABOVE: Giants defensive back Will Blackmon makes a punt return in the first half. PHOTO BY CHRIS FAYTOK

LEFT BOTTOM: Giants defensive end Justin Tuck puts pressure on Jets quarterback Mark Sanchez in the first half. PHOTO BY CHRIS FAYTOK

OPPOSITE: Dan Zoller and Katie Fox of Bridgewater bridge their teams' rivalry with a kiss in the MetLife Stadium parking lot. PHOTO BY ANDREW MILLS

ABOVE: Giants strong safety Kenny Phillips eyes up Jets quarterback Mark Sanchez at the line of scrimmage before a play in the first half, when the Giants outscored the Jets 10-7.
PHOTO BY CHRIS FAYTOK

LEFT: Giants wide receiver Victor Cruz leaps up after being knocked out of bounds by Jets free safety Brodney Pool after Cruz brought in a 36-yard catch in the third quarter. PHOTO BY ANDREW MILLS

BELOW: Giants cornerback Corey Webster delivers a hit on Jets wide receiver Santonio Holmes, jarring the bar loose for an incompletion in the second half. PHOTO BY ANDREW MILLS

OPPOSITE: Giants running back Ahmad Bradshaw stiff-arms Jets cornerback Darrelle Revis after knocking over Jets free safety Brodney Pool for the first of his two touchdowns in the second half. PHOTO BY ANDREW MILLS

LEFT TOP: The trash talking that had gone on the previous week continued after the game, when Jets coach Rex Ryan and Giants running back Brandon Jacobs had a "private conversation." PHOTO BY WILLIAM PERLMAN

LEFT BOTTOM: Giants defensive tackle Chris Canty sacks Jets quarterback Mark Sanchez for a safety in the fourth quarter. PHOTO BY WILLIAM PERLMAN

FINISHING OFF THE COWBOYS

By Mike Garafolo

The theme of this season for Tom Coughlin was simple: "Finish." If he said it once in training camp, he said it a million times since then.

Finish. Finish. Finish.

The Giants did last night — barely. And now, the Cowboys are finished.

The seeming pattern of Coughlin meltdowns, which led to the "finish" theme, was broken by a 31-14 victory at MetLife Stadium last night that wasn't as easy as the final score indicates.

The Giants (9-7) are NFC East champions and will host the Falcons at 1 p.m. Sunday in their first playoff game following a two-year absence from the postseason.

"We straightened it around and finished the game the way we wanted to finish it, finished the regular season the way we wanted to finish it," Coughlin

said, adding four more "finishes" to his season tally, "and created an opportunity for ourselves to be in the playoffs."

After a 6-2 start nearly spiraled downward, the Giants closed with a pair of victories over the rival Jets and Cowboys (8-8) that have them believing they can make a run in the coming weeks.

"I know I've said many times I don't like (the Cowboys) and they don't like me," said Justin Tuck, who had one of the Giants' six sacks. "But you have to respect a team like that."

Especially after they didn't fold following a rare fast start by the Giants. Tuck initially said he was surprised the Giants didn't "finish" (his word, we promise) the Cowboys, but when told this team never seems to make things easy he realized he misspoke.

No, the Giants needed another outstanding late performance by Eli Manning (24-for-33 for 346 yards and three touchdowns), a big stop by Michael Boley and Jason Pierre-Paul on a quarterback sneak early in the fourth quarter and a couple of clutch third-down grabs by Victor Cruz and Hakeem Nicks to fend off a comeback attempt by the Cowboys behind the bruised right hand of quarterback Tony Romo, who hit Laurent Robinson for two touchdowns in the second half to make this a game.

LEFT: Giants running back Ahmad Bradshaw eludes the grasp of Cowboys linebacker Sean Lee as he dives into the end zone for his second touchdown of the second quarter.
PHOTO BY ANDREW MILLS

clutch by going 6-for-8 for 113 yards and a touchdown in the fourth quarter.

"We've been through a lot, definitely some ups and downs," he said. "But to keep our poise, to keep confident, for guys to stick together and not to turn on each other." We came together and knew what we had to do to win the NFC East and we got it accomplished."

Thanks in part to Nicks' 36-yard reception from Manning on a crossing route to convert a third-and-5 with 4:04 to play and move the ball to the Cowboys' 4-yard line. His touchdown catch on the next play, uh, finished the drive and provide the final margin.

Again, it wasn't quite as easy as it looked, though it probably should've been after Cruz's touchdown, which was keyed by a nice block from Nicks on Mike Jenkins, and two nifty touchdowns by Ahmad Bradshaw gave the Giants a 21-0 lead at the half — their biggest advantage of the season and their largest halftime lead since going up 24-3 on the Eagles in Week 15 last season.

That one didn't end so well. Nor did that season.

Thus, the theme this time around — finish — plus a special one for this game to help make it happen.

"Everyone threw in all of their poker chips," said Antrel Rolle, who had an interception in the second half to help slow the Cowboys' comeback. "We're all in." ∎

"There was speculation about Romo's hand," Coughlin said, "which obviously wasn't very accurate."

Cruz's big catch was a 44-yard leaping grab over cornerback Orlando Scandrick on a third-and-7 with 9:22 left in the game and the Giants holding on to a one-touchdown lead. It was the first time the Giants had gained a first down since Manning hit Cruz for 27 yards less than a minute into the second half.

"The defender's in position there," Coughlin said. "But Eli does a great job of avoiding the rush and throws the ball up and Cruz comes down with the ball."

Cruz opened the scoring last night with a 74-yard touchdown on a quick out-and-run, giving him five touchdowns of 68 or more yards this season. The former undrafted free agent became the first NFL player with five or more touchdowns of 65 yards or longer since the Rams' Elroy "Crazy Legs" Hirsch had six in 1951.

However, his fourth-quarter catch might've been more vital because it set up a 28-yard field goal that made it a 10-point game with 5:46 to go.

"Just a heck of a game," Coughlin said, "a heck of a season for the kid."

And for Manning, who once again delivered in the

OPPOSITE: Giants running back Ahmad Bradshaw gets psyched up before the game. PHOTO BY WILLIAM PERLMAN

ABOVE: Giants receiver Victor Cruz grabs a catch and stays out of Cowboys cornerback Orlando Scandrick's grasp in the second half. PHOTO BY TIM FARRELL

RIGHT: Giants defensive end Jason Pierre-Paul sacks Tony Romo, one of six times the Cowboys quarterback was brought down during the game. PHOTO BY WILLIAM PERLMAN

OPPOSITE, LEFT: Giants wide receiver Victor Cruz runs away from Cowboys cornerback Terence Newman and down the field for 74 yards and a first-quarter touchdown. PHOTO BY WILLIAM PERLMAN

OPPOSITE, TOP RIGHT: Giants defensive end Jason Pierre-Paul (90) and middle linebacker Chase Blackburn (93) chase down Cowboys running back Felix Jones in the second half. PHOTO BY CHRIS FAYTOK

OPPOSITE, BOTTOM RIGHT: Cowboys cornerback Orlando Scandrick comes up short as Giants wide receiver Hakeem Nicks grabs a touchdown catch in the fourth quarter. PHOTO BY TIM FARRELL

ABOVE: Giants defensive end Dave Tollefson waves to the crowd as he leaves the field at MetLife Stadium. PHOTO BY TIM FARRELL

RIGHT: Giants running back Brandon Jacobs runs off the field as the stadium screens herald the team's NFC East title. PHOTO BY TIM FARRELL

OPPOSITE: Giants head coach Tom Coughlin gets a postgame bath courtesy of Justin Tuck and Chris Snee to celebrate the team's return to the playoffs for the first time in three years. PHOTO BY CHRIS FAYTOK

A SURGE OF CONFIDENCE

By Mike Garafolo

JUSTIN TUCK COULDN'T EVEN KEEP a straight face and paused for the expected laughter when he turned his postgame news conference into an after-school special.

"I know it's kind of clichéd," the Giants' defensive captain said after the unit technically pitched a shutout in yesterday's 24-2 playoff victory over the Falcons, "but if you believe, you can achieve."

Go ahead, laugh. It's okay.

"Believe" was the theme of Tom Coughlin's speeches to the team last week, and it's not the first time those talks have seemed more like NBC's "The More You Know" public service announcements than NFL pep talks.

But know this team does believe in its head coach, in quarterback Eli Manning, in its pass rush, in the players that have filled in for those who were lost, in the running game and in defensive coordinator

Perry Fewell — some of which might not have been trustworthy at one point or another this season.

And it's showing.

Oh, and in case you were wondering, they believe in their chances against the Packers next Sunday in Lambeau Field — the first playoff game there since Lawrence Tynes kicked the Giants and Coughlin's chapped cheeks to the Super Bowl.

"We're going to win," said All-Pro defensive end Jason Pierre-Paul, who had eight total tackles and shook off a scary collision with Aaron Ross to make one of the two stops on a fourth-down quarterback sneak by Matt Ryan. "A hundred percent we're going to win."

And why's that?

"Because we're the best," he added.

Oh, he believes, all right. And he's not alone. Though few were as outspoken as Pierre-Paul in their confidence about this next matchup with Aaron Rodgers and the almost-perfect Packers — as you'll remember, Green Bay barely edged the Giants, 38-35, here last month — the Giants like what they see.

Manning (23-for-32 for 277 yards and three touchdowns) carried his "elite," record-breaking regular-season form into the playoffs, Hakeem Nicks (72-yard touchdown) reminded everyone drooling

LEFT: Giants wide receiver Hakeem Nicks celebrates his third-quarter touchdown and his second of the lopsided win. PHOTO BY TIM FARRELL

99

Meanwhile, the Falcons' alleged "dirtbag" offensive linemen, Michael Turner and the rest of Atlanta's ball carriers got only 64 yards on 21 attempts.

"We came out today and said, 'You can't run the ball on us,'" Pierre-Paul said.

But the Giants could. And Jacobs' 34-yard run off the right side — behind guard Chris Snee, who had just returned after missing a few plays with what appeared to be a neck burner — set up Nicks' 4-yard touchdown on a play-action pass similar to the one David Tyree caught on a short slant in the end zone in Super Bowl XLII.

"It's not '07!" exclaimed David Diehl, one of a few players tired of the comparisons to that team.

Okay, okay, we get it. Anyway, the Giants took that 7-2 lead, made it 10-2 on a 22-yard field goal by Tynes in the third quarter. Then, Nicks pulled a Cruz by turning a short in cut in to his long touchdown against a confused Falcons secondary (which was without top corner Brent Grimes because of a knee injury) that missed four tackles on the play.

The Giants' next possession was one of their more impressive ones of the season because they went 85 yards on 10 plays, capped with a 27-yard touchdown pass from Manning to Mario Manningham, to make it easy on themselves for once.

"You allow yourself to step back and enjoy it for a minute," Tuck said. "That was a great feeling."

As is believing.

Tuck, who admitted earlier this season he wasn't sure how this team would respond to all of the key players lost to injury in August and September, is finally certain how the team would react to such adversity.

"Right now we have a high level of belief in each other," he said, "and it's showing on the football field." ■

over Victor Cruz he's pretty darn good as well, Ahmad Bradshaw and Brandon Jacobs combined for 155 of the team's season-high 172 rushing yards and Fewell's defense kept the Falcons off the scoreboard.

It was a shutout for Fewell's bunch — sort of. A safety on Manning when he was called for intentional grounding in the end zone to open the scoring in the second quarter made the Falcons the only team in NFL history to score only 2 points in a playoff game.

"Nah, we're a team, man, we're a team," Osi Umenyiora, who had a late sack to give him 10 in 10

games, said when asked if it was a shutout. "Next time, hopefully, it'll be zero."

It's been 28 total in the past three games for the defense. That's a terrific number, considering two of the four touchdowns were scored on short fields for the offense.

The Giants even overcame the loss of Ross, who didn't return after suffering a concussion on that collision in the third quarter. Rookie Prince Amukamara, who hadn't seen the field since struggling against the Cowboys and Redskins, took Ross' spot. Some safety help over the top (with Amukamara a few times actually being the safety) allowed the secondary to hold Ryan to 199 yards on 24-for-41 passing and keep Roddy White and Julio Jones in check.

ABOVE: Giants running back Brandon Jacobs greets fans before the game, played on his home turf, MetLife Stadium.
PHOTO BY CHRIS FAYTOK

LEFT: The Giants' faithful wave "All In" playoff towels during opening kickoff. PHOTO BY ANDREW MILLS

BELOW LEFT: Giants receiver Hakeem Nicks leaps above Falcons cornerback Dominique Franks to make a touchdown catch in the second quarter. PHOTO BY ANDREW MILLS

BELOW RIGHT: Giants cornerback Corey Webster breaks up a pass intended for Falcons wide receiver Roddy White in the second quarter. PHOTO BY ANDREW MILLS

OPPOSITE: Giants receiver Hakeem Nicks puts the Falcons defense on the run during a 72-yard touchdown play late in the third quarter. PHOTO BY TIM FARRELL

ABOVE: Giants wide receiver Mario Mannigham gets past Falcons strong safety James Sanderes to grab a 27-yard pass for a touchdown in the fourth quarter. PHOTO BY CHRIS FAYTOK

ABOVE: Giants defensive end Osi Umenyiora reaches over Falcons tackle Will Svitek to sack quarterback Matt Ryan on a fourth down to effectively end the game. PHOTO BY CHRIS FAYTOK

RIGHT: Giants head coach Tom Coughlin celebrates the fourth-down sack in the final minute of the game. PHOTO BY TIM FARRELL

ABOVE: Giants running back Brandon Jacobs, who rushed for 92 yards on 14 carries, basks in the glow of the wild-card victory. PHOTO BY CHRIS FAYTOK

BLUE CHEESE: ANOTHER UNDERDOG VICTORY

By Mike Garafolo

ON THE DRY-ERASE BOARD INSIDE a jubilant visitors' locker room at Lambeau Field, a simple message was scribbled that pretty much summed up the attitude of the temporary occupants.

"Play physical football," it began. "And beat the hell out of #88."

Nearby, Antrel Rolle was talking to reporters about the paper pinned to his locker. It was a picture of Aaron Rodgers' head with an arrow pointing to a red, cherry-flavored Tootsie Pop. Below it was the word "sucker."

Even during Tom Coughlin's news conference, the most straight-laced coach in the league got as close to puffing his chest out as he'll ever go when he proclaimed, "I think we are a dangerous team."

LEFT: Strong safety Kenny Phillips celebrates the win.
PHOTO BY WILLIAM PERLMAN

Uh, yeah. Everyone knows that by now, especially the no-longer-defending-champion Packers, whose near-perfect season ended with a decisive, 37-20 defeat in yesterday's NFC divisional-round game to a Giants team riding a wave of momentum unlike any they've experienced since early 2008.

They're confident. They're cocky. And after getting revenge for the loss to the Packers last month, they're on their way to a rematch with the 49ers in next weekend's NFC Championship Game.

"This football team will be ready to play. We're going to be hard to beat and that's why we're confident," defensive captain Justin Tuck said. "We know what we have in this room. I know (Jason Pierre-Paul) guaranteed a win and things like that.

"We're very confident. We believe in this football team. If it comes out our words (make it) sound like we're arrogant, I'm sorry."

Tuck claimed very few people gave the Giants a chance to win. He's wrong. Very wrong.

The Giants (11-7) were the trendy pick because they were the hot team and have been doing all of the things that win games this time of year, like getting after the quarterback, running the ball well, playing solid downfield coverage, winning the turnover battle and riding Eli Manning's hot hand.

They did all of the above yesterday and even tossed in a 37-yard Hail Mary touchdown from Manning to Hakeem Nicks on the final play of the first half, following a terrific 23-yard cutback run by Ahmad Bradshaw.

They played physical, they overcame a few injuries and questionable calls and they flustered the "sucker."

That would be Rodgers, the potential league MVP who seemed to be a bit rusty and out-of-synch with his receivers in their first game since Christmas night.

"Oh, it's real," said Rodgers, who was 26-for-46 for 264 yards, two touchdowns and a late interception by Deon Grant that sealed it. "We got beat by a team that played better tonight."

Said Pierre-Paul: "They weren't on their game, but that's not my fault."

It all began with a pace the Giants couldn't have drawn up much better. Like Super Bowl XLII, which they defeated the Patriots 17-14 after losing a 38-35 track meet in the regular season (the same score as the loss to Green Bay last month), they knew they had to slow down yesterday's game and play keep-away from Rodgers.

After the Pack won the opening toss but deferred, the Giants went 67 yards in 13 plays on a drive that lasted 6 minutes, 27 seconds. It ended with a field goal, and the Packers tied it on the next series, but the pace was certainly the right one for the Giants.

However, Nicks put his foot on the gas with a 66-yard touchdown one week after a 72-yarder against the Falcons. Last week, he avoided safety Thomas DeCoud; yesterday, he bounced off a poor shoulder-tackle attempt by former Giants draft pick Charlie Peprah.

"You have to tackle in the playoffs," Peprah said.

You also have to catch the ball and not turn it over. The Packers had six drops, three lost fumbles and the one interception by Grant. John Kuhn's fumble with 3:48 left in the second quarter, which occurred when he ran into one of his blockers, gave the Giants the ball at the Packers' 34. The Giants turned that

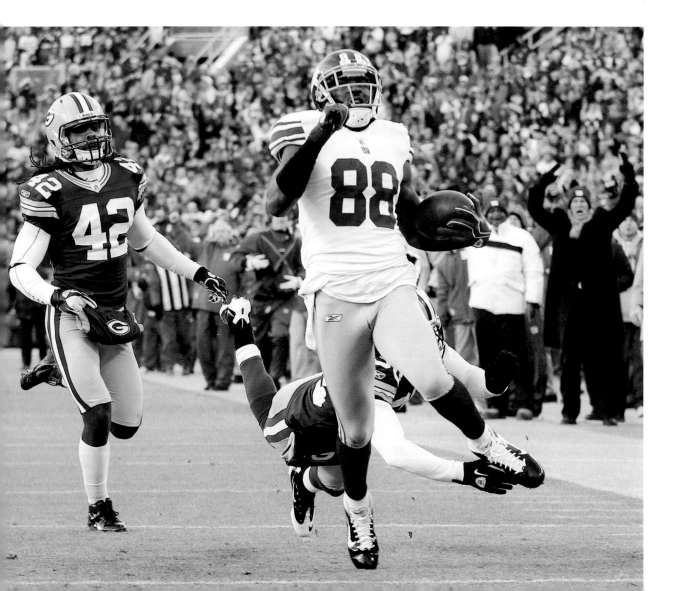

LEFT: Giants wide receiver Hakeem Nicks gets by Packers free safety Morgan Burnett and cornerback Tramon Williams for a first-quarter touchdown. PHOTO BY ANDREW MILLS

OPPOSITE: Packers fullback John Kuhn goes airborne over Giants cornerback Aaron Ross and into the end zone of the first play of the second quarter. PHOTO BY ANDREW MILLS

into a field goal and a 13-10 lead. A sack by Michael Boley gave them the ball back at their own 31 with 41 seconds left in the second quarter.

Seemingly content to head into the locker room with a three-point lead, the Giants ran a draw play. The Packers called timeout at the snap, so they lined up and ran a toss left to Bradshaw. Pretty soon, he was on the right sideline and well downfield.

Bradshaw looked to see there were 15 seconds on the clock before the play, so knew he had time to pick up as much yardage as possible before getting out of bounds.

"It was a shock to see him over there," right guard Chris Snee said. "But he makes plays."

Instead of attempting a 55-yard field goal, Coughlin opted for the "flood tip" Hail Mary that Nicks caught off his face mask with Charles Woodson covering. Coughlin saw Nicks' 4-XL gloves appear in mid-air and immediately knew he had a good shot to bring it down.

"That gave us a huge lift right there," Coughlin said. "It's one or two times a year that play is completed and fortunately for us it was completed tonight."

Green Bay pulled within a touchdown but a failed fourth-and-5 early in the fourth quarter followed by a Giants field goal extended the lead to 23-13 with 7:48 to play.

Kenny Phillips' forced fumble on Don Bosco grad Ryan Grant, a recovery and return to the 4-yard line by Chase Blackburn and Manning's touchdown to Manningham had Phillips and Rolle doing a sideline shimmy together. The Giants' sideline was celebrating but surprisingly calm, as if they fully expected this to happen.

Which it did. Now, in the words of the late rapper Notorious B.I.G., and as a few players sang on their way into the locker room, they're "going, going, back,

back to Cali, Cali," where they lost 27-20 in Week 10.

"We're happy as hell about this win. But we're thinking," Snee said. "We have greater plans. We're thinking about next week, what that atmosphere will be like.

"You saw it on TV; (Candlestick Park) was rockin' and they were hitting. So it'll be a very physical game." ∎

OPPOSITE: Giants quarterback Eli Manning throws on the run with Packers linebacker Brad Jones bearing down on him in the first half. Manning threw for the 330 yards and three touchdowns. PHOTO BY ANDREW MILLS

ABOVE: Giants strong safety Kenny Phillips picks up the loose ball on the apparent fumble by Packers wide receiver Greg Jennings as he is tackled by strong safety Deon Grant. It was ruled a down by contact. PHOTO BY WILLIAM PERLMAN

OPPOSITE: Giants tight end Jake Ballard makes a 17-yard catch for a first down in the second quarter. PHOTO BY ANDREW MILLS

ABOVE: Giants cornerback Corey Webster and outside linebacker Michael Boley take down Packers quarterback Aaron Rodgers, who was sacked four times. PHOTO BY WILLIAM PERLMAN

RIGHT: Mario Manningham, with coach Tom Coughlin in the second half, finished the game with 31 yards on three receptions and one touchdown.
PHOTO BY ANDREW MILLS

OPPOSITE: Giants defensive end Osi Umenyiora competes with Packers quarterback Aaron Rodgers tackle Chad Clifton for a fumble.
PHOTO BY WILLIAM PERLMAN

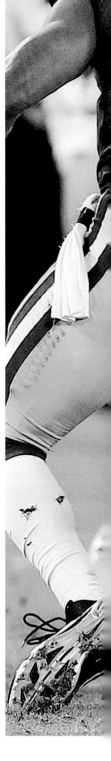

OPPOSITE: Giants free safety Antrel Rolle, who had eight tackles and one fumble recovery, begins the celebration. PHOTO BY ANDREW MILLS

ABOVE: Even in Green Bay, there was Giants blue to be found. The dedicated fans who made the trek included Joe Ruback, of New City, N.Y., aka License Plate Guy. PHOTO BY WILLIAM PERLMAN

LEFT: Giants quarterback Eli Manning leaves Lambeau Field, after his second upset playoff win.
PHOTO BY WILLIAM PERLMAN

19 DOWN, 1 TO GO

By Mike Garafolo

STEVE WEATHERFORD, HAVING FIELDED A low snap and put down the most important hold of his life, was now celebrating inside the cramped, joyous visitors' locker room at Candlestick Park.

Wearing only a towel, he climbed the short wall next to his locker and looked like a wrestler going off the top ropes.

"We're going to the Super Bowl!" the Giants' punter yelled as he landed on screaming, somewhat-frightened equipment manager Joe Skiba.

It was that kind of scene inside this throwback locker room, in this throwback stadium, after a throwback game the Giants won, 20-17, against the 49ers on another overtime field goal by Lawrence Tynes. This one, set up by a clutch forced fumble by rookie Jacquian Williams, was a 31-yarder that sailed through the uprights with 7:06 left in the extra session, giving the Giants their fifth NFC Championship Game victory in as many tries and sending them to Indianapolis in 13 days for a rematch with the Patriots in Super Bowl XLVI.

LEFT: Giants quarterback Eli Manning calls out the protection during the first half of the NFC Championship Game between the Giants and the San Francisco 49ers at Candlestick Park. PHOTO BY CHRIS FAYTOK

Justin Tuck couldn't bring himself to watch the kick after a delay-of-game penalty pushed Tynes back 5 yards and a timeout made this excruciatingly tight game that much more riveting — or gut-wrenching.

"I couldn't take it," the defensive captain said. "I had to turn around and look, and I was glad to see what I saw."

What he saw was bedlam on the field: Weatherford running toward the sideline and yelling "Super Bowl!" with a few choice words tucked in there, Tynes looking for his wife, Amanda, players embracing and the tightest squeeze toward a locker room in the NFL.

In that hallway in the southeast end of the stadium, in which Eli Manning had only slightly more room to operate than he did in his own backfield all night long, the Giants quarterback bumped into misty-eyed 49ers coach Jim Harbaugh.

"Congratulations," Harbaugh said. "Go win it. Go win it."

They won this one, thanks to the kind of things Tom Coughlin preached from the first day of training camp through the final practice before this one: protect the football, win the turnover battle and don't make mental mistakes.

With these offenses stuck in neutral for the final 5:39 of regulation, following a 25-yard field goal by David Akers that tied the game, it was pretty clear a mistake would be the difference. The Giants hadn't turned the ball over all game, so they were confident

was stopped at the end of a 6-yard gain on second-and-21 before the ball was pried loose. The 49ers recovered, but it didn't matter because it's a judgment call and it can't be challenged.

It's the second time the Giants benefitted from that rule in this building this season. Back in Week 10, Victor Cruz's progress was stopped before a fumble.

Not so for the Williams-on-Williams fumble in overtime.

Jacquian said, at first, he was trying to make a tackle. But once Kyle made a cut, he took a shot at the ball.

And got all of it.

"I always dreamed of making a big play," Jacquian said.

Funny, because Tynes dreamed of making the winning kick the night before. So while Bradshaw was trying to "hit my head on the goalpost," meaning score a touchdown instead of settling for a field goal in overtime, Tynes knew it would come down to him.

Weatherford, meanwhile, was steaming. At least, Coughlin thought he was.

"He looked like he was upset. I was trying to figure out what was wrong," Coughlin said of Weatherford, who had been on the losing side of the previous two AFC Championship games with the Jets. "And he said, 'I want to get this field goal kicked and go to the Super Bowl.' I said, 'That sounds like a good idea to me.'"

From idea to execution, it happened, thanks in part to Weatherford's scoop of the low snap by Zak DeOssie.

"I knew if I got the ball down and the laces out, Lawrence Tynes was going to make the kick and we were going to Indianapolis for the Super Bowl," Weatherford said. "We did it." ∎

their style of football would prevail.

"That was the thing I kept telling myself, 'Be patient, don't force anything, don't give them anything, our defense is playing well,'" said Manning, who shook off six sacks to go 32-for-58 for 316 yards with two touchdowns, including a beauty to Mario Manningham in the fourth quarter that gave the Giants a 17-14 lead. "We stuck with that and got some turnovers."

None bigger than Williams' strip of another Williams — 49ers returner Kyle Williams was taking the place of injured Ted Ginn Jr. — that was recovered by veteran Devin Thomas at the 49ers' 24-yard line.

Earlier, Kyle Williams had a bouncing punt barely nick his knee. A replay challenge by the Giants confirmed as much, and Thomas' recovery on that one set up Manningham's touchdown.

Perhaps rattled, the Giants had a feeling they could force Williams to make a mistake, especially while carrying a slick ball.

"He's had a lot of concussions. We were just like, 'We gotta put a hit on that guy,'" Thomas said. "(Tyler) Sash did a great job hitting him early and he looked kind of dazed when he got up. I feel like that made a difference and he coughed it up."

Coughlin had reminded the players "pretty much the entire week" about protecting the ball (offense) and trying to take it away (defense). He had a brief lump-in-throat moment, for sure, when Ahmad Bradshaw coughed it up at the Giants' 21-yard line with slightly more than two minutes left in regulation.

But the officials ruled Bradshaw's forward progress

LEFT: 49ers tight end Vernon Davis stays in bounds for a 73-yard touchdown catch and run in the first quarter. PHOTO BY ANDREW MILLS

OPPOSITE: Candlestick Park grounds crew members work feverishly to clear water from the field during pregame warmups. PHOTO BY ANDREW MILLS

BELOW LEFT: Giants outside linebacker Michael Boley battles with 49ers offensive tackle Anthony Davis, a Piscataway native, in the first half. PHOTO BY CHRIS FAYTOK

BELOW RIGHT: 49ers wide receiver Kyle Williams and offensive guard Mike Lupati go after the loose ball with Giants defensive end Osi Umenyiora. PHOTO BY WILLIAM PERLMAN

FOLLOWING LEFT: Giants tight end Bear Pascoe puts his shoulder down and drives 49ers free safety Dashon Goldson into the end zone for a Giants touchdown in the second quarter. PHOTO BY ANDREW MILLS

FOLLOWING RIGHT: Giants wide receiver Victor Cruz makes a leaping catch as 49ers cornerback Carlos Rogers trails during the first half. PHOTO BY CHRIS FAYTOK

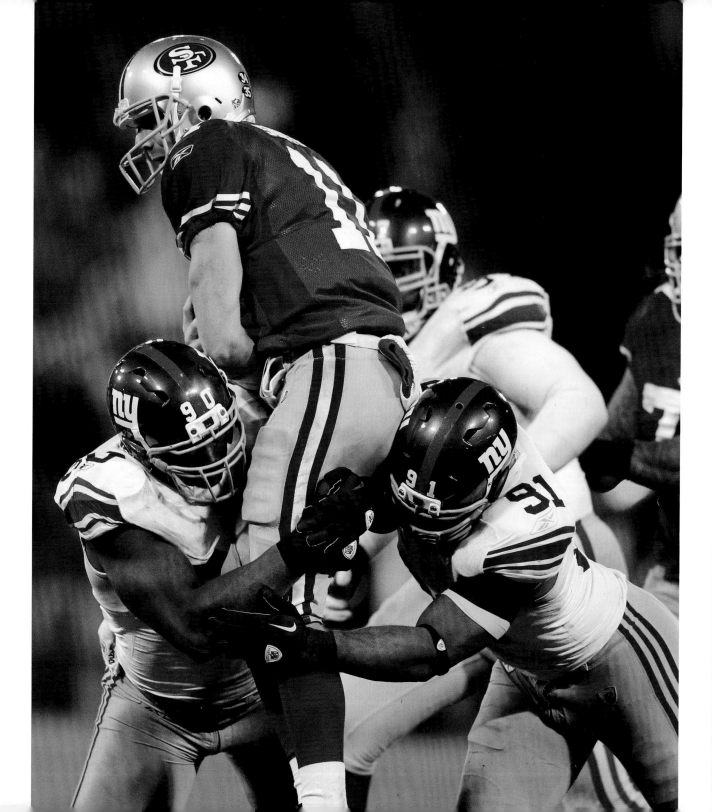

RIGHT: Giants defensive ends Jason Pierre-Paul and Justin Tuck combine to sack 49ers quarterback Alex Smith during the fourth quarter.
PHOTO BY CHRIS FAYTOK

FAR RIGHT: Giants running back Ahmad Bradshaw tries to get past 49ers cornerback Carlos Rogers and free safety Dashon Goldson during the third quarter.
PHOTO BY CHRIS FAYTOK

ABOVE RIGHT: Giants strong safety Kenny Phillips breaks up the catch of 49ers tight end Vernon Davis.
PHOTO BY WILLIAM PERLMAN

BELOW RIGHT: Eli Manning gets hit hard and is sacked in the second half.
PHOTO BY ANDREW MILLS

FAR RIGHT: With the team trailing 14-10 at the start of the fourth quarter, the Giants defense comes together.
PHOTO BY ANDREW MILLS

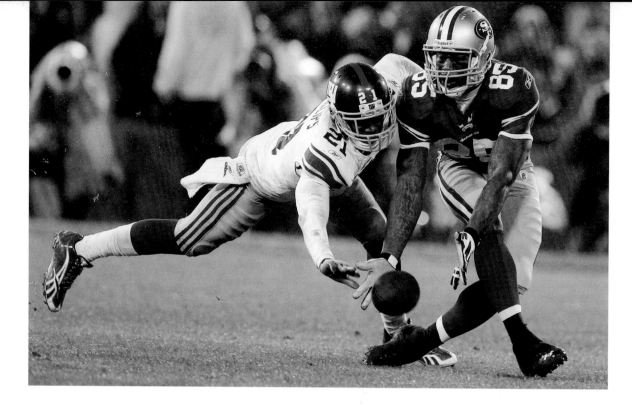

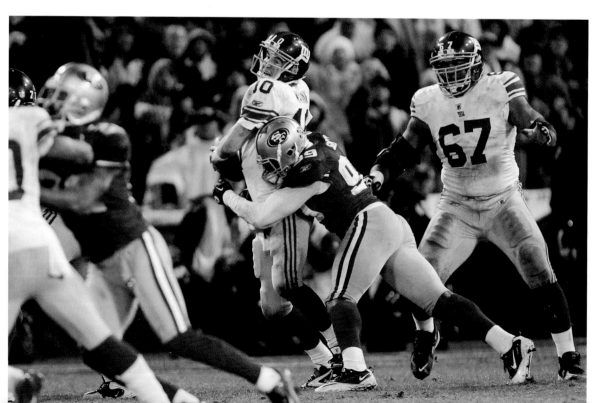

GIANTS
10
T.O.L.
3
BALL ON
45
QTR
4
usbank
WELCOME TO
BILL WALSH FIELD
49ERS
SASH
39
PAYSINGER
55
KIWANUKA
94

LEFT: Giants wide receiver Mario Manningham beats 49ers defensive back Tramaine Brock to make the go-ahead touchdown catch in the fourth quarter. PHOTO BY ANDREW MILLS

OPPOSITE: Giants middle linebacker Jacquian Williams strips the ball from 49ers punt returner Kyle Williams in OT. PHOTO BY ANDREW MILLS

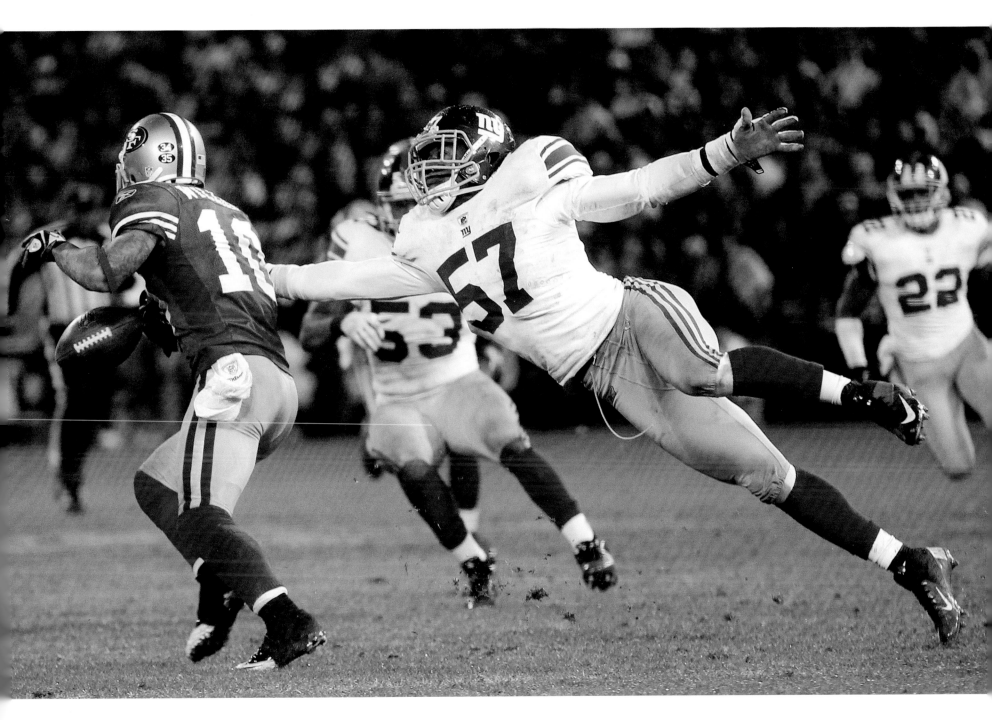

FAR LEFT: Giants kicker Lawrence Tynes and punter Steve Weatherford rejoice after a field goal send the Giants to Indianapolis.
PHOTO BY WILLIAM PERLMAN

ABOVE: Lawrence Tynes finds his wife, Amanda, after his field goal.
PHOTO BY WILLIAM PERLMAN

LEFT: Giants kicker Lawrence Tynes celebrates his game-winning field goal with quarterback Eli Manning.
PHOTO BY CHRIS FAYTOK

PATRIOTS

Blue Heaven

Giants grab the glory again in a brilliant repeat performance

By Mike Garafolo

INDIANAPOLIS — JOHN MARA STOOD on the sideline, confetti strewn around his feet as he waited for a live television shot to begin. The fans nearby in the front rows of Lucas Oil Stadium were chanting, "Déjà Blue! Déjà Blue!"

The Giants co-owner had experienced this all before, everything up to the Hail Mary pass from Tom Brady that stole Mara's breath because it looked for a moment like it might be completed.

Yet somehow, it all seemed unbelievable.

"Did we just win the Super Bowl?" Mara said with a laugh and a head shake.

They most certainly did, 21-17 over the New England Patriots. A familiar foe. Defeated in familiar fashion.

Eli Manning, as himself, led another winning touchdown drive, an 88-yarder that began with 3:46 remaining. Mario Manningham was David Tyree, sparking the drive with an incredible 38-yard, toe-

tapping catch up the left sideline on a perfect throw from Manning. Ahmad Bradshaw was Plaxico Burress, scoring the decisive points — though this one wasn't nearly as stylish. Bradshaw's 6-yarder ended with him falling backward into the end zone with 57 seconds left, unable to stop at the 1-yard line as he'd been instructed.

Justin Tuck played the role of Jay Alford with a sack of Brady on the Pats' final desperation drive. And Kenny Phillips was this year's Corey Webster, tipping away that pass from Brady to Aaron Hernandez in the end zone, ending the game, igniting the celebration and allowing Mara to finally believe.

"To get one Super Bowl win in the manner we got it four years ago usually lasts a whole career," Mara said. "But to get two of these is just beyond description."

Mara was happy for everyone, but most of all for his coach Tom Coughlin, whom he hoped will "finally be appreciated the way he should be appreciated."

That's now two rings for Coughlin, who fell in love with this team — literally. He told the players Saturday night he loved them.

Right after he reminded them once again to finish.

"This is the finish line for this year," Coughlin said in reference to the team mantra that began in training camp. "Yes it is!"

Upon crossing that line, Jason Pierre-Paul dropped to a knee, lowered his head and prayed. Rookie Jacquian Williams took a seat on the goal line and

---

LEFT: Brandon Jacobs leads the team in a pregame pep talk. PHOTO BY JOHN MUNSON

It didn't seem fair to some a team that was, as Mara put it, "just trying to survive at 7-7" could become the first Super Bowl champion with fewer than 10 regular-season victories. But that's how it works in today's NFL, and the Giants rode momentum to a season-ending six-game winning streak — and another Lombardi Trophy.

"New York vs. Boston, are you kidding me? For all the gold?" Brandon Jacobs said. "And we came up with it again."

Said team chairman Steve Tisch: "I thought four years ago was exciting. That was a dress rehearsal."

Just like that game, this one began with solid defense from the Giants. Tuck helped open the scoring by forcing Brady to throw a ball deep down the middle of the field to nobody. It was ruled intentional grounding in the end zone for a safety.

Cruz then capped an incredible story of this season with a 2-yard touchdown on a quick slant just past Pats linebacker Jerod Mayo. That came shortly after Cruz fumbled, only to be saved by a penalty on the Pats for too many men on the field.

"I had to bobble that a little bit," Cruz said. "But once I got it, I snagged it and then it was salsa time, baby!"

Pretty soon, the Patriots began dancing through the Giants' secondary. Brady, in the midst of a Super Bowl-record 16 straight completions, led touchdown drives of 96 and 79 yards on either side of halftime. Added to a field goal earlier, it gave New England a 17-9 lead less than 4 minutes into the second half.

"We got out of doing what we do. We started trying to make too many plays," Giants safety Deon Grant said, adding: "I told the guys at halftime, 'Muhammad Ali got hit. You're going to get hit in a fight. He's still the champ, still the greatest ever.'"

The Giants are champs again because of 12 unanswered points, starting with two field goals by Lawrence Tynes. The defense was simultaneously

leaned back on his hands, trying to figure out if it was a dream.

Chase Blackburn, almost a substitute teacher in November and a key to this victory with an interception of Brady 49 yards down the field, did a few interviews near Manning's new Corvette (for being named MVP after completing 30 of 40 passes for 296 yards and a touchdown to Victor Cruz) before he had to put his kids to bed.

ABOVE: Running backs Brandon Jacobs and Ahmad Bradshaw get ready for the game in the end zone.
PHOTO BY CHRIS FAYTOK

Tyree gave a big hug to Cruz and spoke about Manningham's catch, saying, "You've gotta have a playmaker down the stretch." Zak DeOssie, realizing he'd just eclipsed his father in Super Bowl titles, yelled out, "That's my second! Now where's my old man?!" And rapper Flavor Flav , known for wearing a big clock around his neck, was asked what time it was and replied, "Time to get this parade started!"

Meanwhile, it was much less festive outside of the Patriots' locker room. The loudest sound was the hum of the electric lights, as Gisele Bundchen, aka Mrs. Tom Brady, told Vince Wilfork's wife, Bianca, she couldn't take that ending, and Mrs. Wilfork replied, "It's worse for you. … It's not fair."

clamping down, with Blackburn recording his interception on a deep ball to Gronkowski two plays into the fourth quarter. In fact, the Patriots were held scoreless for the final 26-plus minutes of the game.

Finally, it once again came down to Manning leading a winning drive.

It began with the strike to Manningham up the left sideline past rookie corner Sterling Moore. (The Patriots challenged the call, but the great catch was confirmed.) Then, a 16-yarder to Manningham in front of Moore, a quick slant to Hakeem Nicks into a blitz, Bradshaw for 7 yards and Nicks on a "now" route at the line for a first down at the 7-yard line with 1:09 to play.

When Bradshaw then split the defense two plays later, he tried to stop.

"As (Manning) was handing off the ball, he was like, 'Don't score, don't score,' " said Bradshaw, who had 72 yards on 17 carries. "It clicked at the 1-yard line."

Too late.

Actually, too late for the Patriots, who had to go 80 yards in 57 seconds.

Tuck's sack ensured it wouldn't happen.

"Eli's going to steal my MVP again," Tuck said he thought to himself.

Yeah, but walking through the confetti, the last player on the way to the locker room, was quite the consolation prize.

Even if he, like Mara, hadn't quite grasped it all yet.

"It's fitting," said Tuck, who has battled injuries and lost three family members. "Having the year I've had, I'm just tremendously blessed. It really hasn't sunk in yet how great this is.

"Sometime tonight, I'll probably break down and cry in my bed." ∎

ABOVE: Tom Brady is taken down by Justin Tuck after releasing the ball on the Patriots' first play, which was ruled a safety. PHOTO BY ANDREW MILLS

LEFT: The Patriots' Tom Brady launches the ball down the field during the first quarter. The play was called intentional grounding and ruled a safety. PHOTO BY CHRIS FAYTOK

ABOVE: Victor Cruz catches a first-quarter touchdown, putting the Giants ahead 9-0. PHOTO BY WILLIAM PERLMAN

RIGHT: Victor Cruz celebrates with his signature salsa dance. PHOTO BY ANDREW MILLS

BELOW: Punter Steve Weatherford and Aaron Ross celebrate Weatherford's second-quarter punt inside the 5-yard line. PHOTO BY JOHN MUNSON

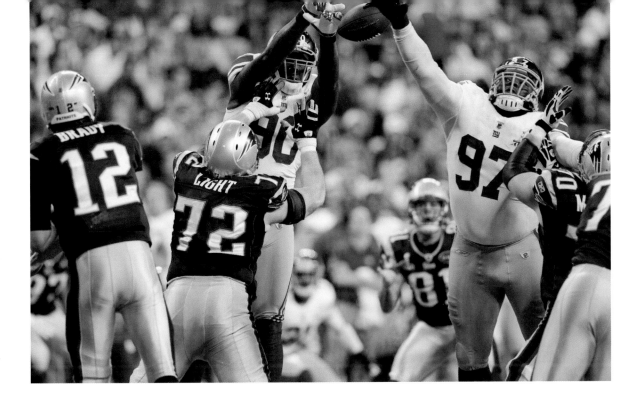

ABOVE: Giants wide receiver Hakeem Nicks makes the catch as he is defended by Patriots cornerback Antwaun Molden. PHOTO BY WILLIAM PERLMAN

ABOVE LEFT: The Giants' Jason Pierre-Paul and Linval Joseph go up to block a Tom Brady pass during the second quarter. PHOTO BY CHRIS FAYTOK

BELOW LEFT: The Patriots' Danny Woodhead celebrates a second-quarter touchdown. PHOTO BY ANDREW MILLS

Victory cements a quarterback's legacy

By Steve Politi

INDIANAPOLIS — HE HAS THE keys to a city now, maybe the keys to the Hall of Fame someday, and certainly the keys to a legacy unrivaled among New York quarterbacks.

But the keys to his new Corvette?

His 10-month-old daughter, Ava, had turned them into a very expensive teething toy. Eli Manning had handed them to her just minutes after he was named the Super Bowl MVP again — the hot ride comes with

the award — and Ava promptly started gnawing away, oblivious to the wild scene around her.

"You've got a new car," Eli told his daughter as he walked through the hallways at Lucas Oil Stadium. "All right!"

Ava was wearing a blue checkered dress decorated with footballs and a bright red bow in her hair that matched her pudgy cheeks. The confetti was still drifting through the air after the 21-17 Giants win, the crowd still buzzing over what they had just witnessed, and Manning wanted to hold his daughter more than the Lombardi Trophy he had won again for his franchise.

His wife, Abby, tried to pass Ava to him, but she reached back to her mommy. Dad just smiled and gave her her a kiss and watched as she promptly dropped those Corvette keys on the ground.

This is the moment that solidifies Eli among the all-time greats, the victory that gives him as many titles as Bart Starr and Roger Staubach, as John Elway and Bob Griese — all Hall of Famers. That he has twice defeated a man with three championships, a quarterback who was supposed to be the greatest of his generation, makes it even more impressive.

Twice now, with more than 100 million people watching, Eli Manning has outplayed Patriots quarterback Tom Brady. Twice now, with a chance to deliver a trophy to the franchise that made a 2004 draft-day trade to acquire him, Manning has rallied the Giants for a thrilling victory.

That's how this game is remembered, how Eli came to Indianapolis and won his second title in the city where his brother Peyton became a legend. How he took the Giants 88 yards in the final 3:46 for the game-winning touchdown, a drive made possible by another incredible catch on a long pass.

Not that Eli was willing to admit any of this, of course.

"I don't think that's the story," he said in his typical humble fashion. "I think the story is that the New York Giants are world champions. That's what I'm proud of. That's all that matters tonight."

So a season that started with Manning lumping himself in Brady's class ended with him outclassing him. It is funny to think back to August, when he made those comments in that radio interview, that there actually was a debate over whether he deserved to be called elite.

"I consider myself in that class," Manning said, then he threw for almost 5,000 yards, led the Giants to an NFL record six fourth-quarter comebacks, and rallied them from 7-7 into the postseason. But what happened in January and beyond is what cements a legacy for a quarterback, and Manning was near perfect in four playoff wins.

He completed 65 percent of his passes in those victories for 1,219 yards, nine touchdowns and — most importantly — just one interception. He has been so good late in games that, when Brady failed to convert on a third down with four minutes to go and the Patriots had to punt, you knew what would happen next.

"That's Eli," receiver Mario Manningham said. "He's cool as the other side of the pillow. You know he's going to make plays. We've just got to be in a position to back him up."

Manningham did that on the first play of the winning drive, somehow keeping both feet in bounds on a 38-yard sideline strike that put the ball at midfield. It wasn't quite as remarkable as David Tyree's catch four years ago, but it was every bit as important. And the throw, like so many that left his right hand in this game, was perfect.

From there, Manning had to move the Giants and manage the clock. A 16-yard strike to Manningham and a 14-yarder to Hakeem Nicks got the Giants into field-goal range. The Giants had a first-and-goal at the 7 with 69 seconds left, and when the Patriots let running back Ahmad Bradshaw skate into the end zone, Manning was yelling to his teammate, "Don't score! Don't score!"

Bradshaw did score, and that left Manning in the exact position he feared: Standing on the sideline, helpless, watching Brady work. Brady converted a long fourth down and moved the Patriots to midfield, and Manning turned away and clenched his fists.

A few of the assistant coaches joined hands as the final Hail Mary went into the air, but Manning just stood with his hands on his hips, watching the ball soar through the air. The photographers crept closer and closer, and when the football hit the ground, he took off running onto the field.

He found Justin Tuck, the defensive hero, for a bear hug. If you were to pick two players who helped will this team to their two titles, it would be these two — contemporaries who are immortals for this franchise already, with plenty of football in their careers left to play.

That is the question now with Eli Manning: How many more of these can he win? How high can he build his legacy as a winner? Seven of the 10 other starting quarterbacks with two or more championships are enshrined in Canton.

"I know one thing, Eli might have said earlier in the year that he belonged with the elite quarterbacks," his father, Archie Manning, said, "but he will not be saying that he belongs in the Hall of Fame."

He doesn't have to say it. Manning is 31, in the middle of his prime, a two-time Super Bowl MVP already. He can even drive his new Corvette in the ticker-tape parade, if his daughter ever stops chewing on the keys. ■

LEFT: Eli Manning unloads a pass during the second quarter. PHOTO BY CHRIS FAYTOK

OPPOSITE: Eli Manning holds his daughter, Ava, and walks with his wife, Abby, after the game. PHOTO BY ANDREW MILLS

ABOVE: Hakeem Nicks is hit hard by Patrick Chung in the third quarter.
PHOTO BY ANDREW MILLS

LEFT: Giants defensive end Jason Pierre-Paul is attended to by trainers and Tom Coughlin, right, in the third quarter.
PHOTO BY ANDREW MILLS

FAR LEFT: The Patriots' Aaron Hernandez runs down the field to score a touchdown during the third quarter, the Patriots' last points of the game. PHOTO BY CHRIS FAYTOK

ABOVE: Giants head coach Tom Coughlin shouts after the officials failed to call an apparent pass interference in the fourth quarter. PHOTO BY WILLIAM PERLMAN

LEFT: Chase Blackburn celebrates his fourth-quarter interception with defensive coordinator Perry Fewell. PHOTO BY JOHN MUNSON

OPPOSITE: The Giants' Chase Blackburn makes an interception as Rob Gronkowski tries to knock the ball out in the fourth quarter. PHOTO BY ANDREW MILLS

ABOVE AND LEFT: Ahmad Bradshaw tries not to score, but falls into the end zone for a touchdown late in the fourth quarter to give the Giants the lead. PHOTOS BY CHRIS FAYTOK

OPPOSITE: Giants wide receiver Mario Manningham keeps his feet in bounds to make a key 38-yard catch in front of the Patriots' Patrick Chung, left, and Sterling Moore. PHOTO BY CHRIS FAYTOK

In the end, Tuck takes charge

By Dave D'Alessandro

INDIANAPOLIS — For all intents and purposes, Tom Brady's date with destiny began with No. 91 boring in on him like a demonic rhino on his first snap of the game and ended with No. 91 eating him up and spitting him out on the 14-yard line with 36 seconds left in the game.

Count us among those who had a pretty good idea this was coming. And you would have as well — you only had to open your eyes, about 20 minutes before kickoff.

The game hadn't even begun, yet there were 68,000 people who, in fact, knew exactly what kind of attitude Justin Tuck had brought to Super Bowl XLVI.

The Giants' defensive end had assembled a few dozen of his closest friends in the left corner of the south end zone, and for about 7 minutes, he held them spellbound.

They surrounded him in a circle — six, seven deep. He pointed at every single face that stared back at him. "You don't have a ring!" he began, literally shouting at guys like Chris Canty and Michael Boley. "You don't know how this feels. Think about that. Think about what you've missed in your life."

He swung around, his eyes ablaze, his expression an electric glaze, staring at others and not skipping a beat. He raised his forefinger again.

"You know what this is about! You've done this

before!" he shouted at guys like Kenny Phillips and Chase Blackburn. "Remember what being a champion felt like! Think about what it could be like to feel that way again!"

By then, they were feeling the adrenaline rising from the soles of their feet to their extremities, and he hadn't even sung the chorus yet. Did he have their attention? Silly question.

"Oh, yes," said Linval Joseph, the kid who lines up next to Tuck at left tackle. "Everyone listens when Justin talks."

It was a moment a captain lives for. And let the record show that this was the soundtrack for the fourth straight superb performance for this Giants defense, because the 21-17 triumph over the New England Patriots might have been inspired by a pregame rant that drew raves.

"I said, 'None of you want to walk off this field tonight thinking you missed this opportunity, because you never know when you'll get another,' " Tuck explained later. "And I told them that we're built for this. To go out and grab it. It's there for us."

This is the game that lays emotions bare for an audience of billions, and we get each twitch in close-up. He who twitches least usually wins the most, and for the most part, Tuck is one of those guys who has perfected the man-in-the-iron-mask facade.

But on this day, he decided the chuck it. And his team was better off for it.

Of course this game had to come down to defense. Of course it had to come down to getting stops on Brady, and making the Patriots quarterback feel the pressure like it was a swarm of locusts.

But it came down to hearing their captain's message — loud and clear, zero distortion.

"I'll never forget it, really," Joseph said. "He said, 'They're not built like us. We're a one-of-a-kind team. We're a different breed.' "

The kid smiled.

"He's a special leader," he said of Tuck, "for a special team."

This game was played about two hours to the south of his beloved alma mater, Notre Dame, so in a lot of ways it was a special night for Tuck. And make no mistake, it wasn't always easy to keep the faith. The defensive front did not exactly maintain much pressure on Brady throughout this game, but the guys up front did make the plays they needed to make.

It was almost the season in microcosm: inconsistent, shaky, but ultimately dominant. Ultimately, they've earned it. Holding the Pats' offense to 17 points is a great night's work. A perfect ending to an imperfect season.

"It wasn't that we didn't believe we couldn't do this," Tuck explained. "At the time, we weren't playing well, and to get here, you have to play well. I'm blessed to have teammates who step up — we played well together."

It could have come apart, if not for the locker room leadership that guys like this showed in the lean times.

And, perhaps most important, he showed that even the leaders can take constructive criticism. It wasn't long ago that Antrel Rolle called him out — funny how the defense has been a clenched fist ever since — and Tuck never took that personally. There was a reason for that: What's good for any underachiever is good for the captain.

"But through the ups and downs this team has never wavered, never pointed a finger," he said. "Even when we said some things, it was taken the right way. It was taken as motivation. It wasn't being negative, it was guys saying, 'I see this and we need to do it better.' And guys took it the right way, and put a lot of pressure on themselves to play better."

It was about that time that Rolle stuck his head in the postgame scrum, chirping happily, "What's up, Tuck?"

"Be humble, baby — I'm a world champion," the captain replied, without skipping a beat. "You are too, boy."

Again. And judging by the look on his face, the feeling never gets old. ∎

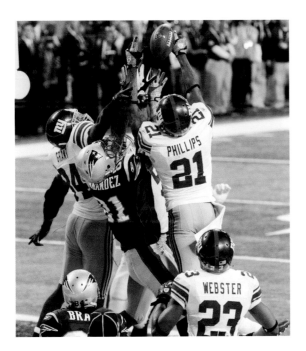

LEFT: The Giants' Deon Grant and Kenny Phillips knock the ball away from the Patriots' Aaron Hernandez on the last play of the game to seal the Giants Super Bowl victory. PHOTO BY TIM FARRELL

OPPOSITE: Justin Tuck, right, celebrates a sack during the last drive of the game. PHOTO BY CHRIS FAYTOK

RIGHT: Giants tight end Jake Ballard, who injured his leg in the second half, does an interview near the cart that brought him back onto the field to watch the final plays. PHOTO BY CHRIS FAYTOK

BELOW LEFT: Derrick Martin plays with his daughters, five-month-old Dash and Harlow Kingsley, 2, in the confetti after the game. PHOTO BY CHRIS FAYTOK

BELOW RIGHT: Giants wide receivers Victor Cruz, Mario Manningham and Hakeem Nicks hold up the trophy. PHOTO BY ANDREW MILLS

ABOVE: Giants coach Tom Coughlin celebrates with his second Vince Lombardi Trophy. PHOTO BY ANDREW MILLS

LEFT: After celebrating with teammates, Justin Tuck takes a knee to steal a quiet moment after the game. PHOTO BY ANDREW MILLS

BELOW: Giants offensive guard Mitch Petrus, left, wide receiver Ramses Barden and guard David Diehl hold the Vince Lombardi Trophy. PHOTO BY WILLIAM PERLMAN

FOLLOWING LEFT: Eli Manning was named the game MVP, the second time he won the honors. PHOTO BY ANDREW MILLS

FOLLOWING RIGHT: Zak DeOssie holds up a Super Bowl champions towel. PHOTO BY ANDREW MILLS

ABOVE: Eli Manning rides with coach Tom Coughlin, members of team ownership and Mayor Michael Bloomberg during the parade up the Canyon of Heroes along Broadway in Lower Manhattan. PHOTO BY JOHN MUNSON

RIGHT: Huge crowds wait for the players during the victory ticker-tape parade. PHOTO BY ANDREW MILLS

FAR RIGHT: Construction workers take a break to watch the ticker-tape parade in honor of the Super Bowl XLVI Champions. PHOTO BY JENNIFER BROWN

LEFT: Giants' wide receiver Victor Cruz has a rooting section in an office building in the Canyon of Heroes.
PHOTO BY TIM FARRELL

BELOW LEFT: Victor Cruz does the salsa on stage with former Giant Michael Strahan at City Hall.
PHOTO BY WILLIAM PERLMAN

BELOW RIGHT: The first float of the parade carries Victor Cruz and Hakeem Nicks up the Canyon of Heroes.
PHOTO BY TIM FARRELL

ABOVE: Thousands of fans pile up at the gate waiting to enter the event celebrating the Giants Super Bowl win over the New England Patriots at MetLife Stadium. PHOTO BY TONY KURDZUK

OPPOSITE TOP: Giants' kicker Larence Tynes and punter Steve Weatherford, right, jumped off their float and joined in with one of the marching bands. PHOTO BY JENNIFER BROWN

OPPOSITE BOTTOM LEFT: Defensive end Justin Tuck, head coach Tom Coughlin (holding the Vince Lombardi Trophy) and QB Eli Manning during the New York Giants Super Bowl XLVI victory parade in New York City. PHOTO BY ANDREW MILLS

OPPOSITE BOTTOM RIGHT: Giants running back Brandon Jacobs dances as Andre Brown starts up the song "I Got a Ring" at City Hall at the New York Giants Super Bowl Victory Parade. PHOTO BY WILLIAM PERLMAN

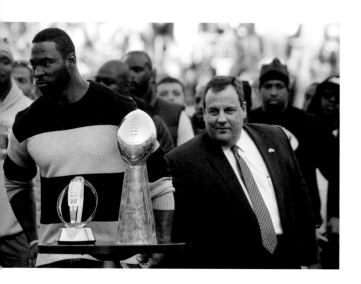

ABOVE: New Jersey Gov. Chris Christie eyes the Vince Lombardi and NFC Championship trophies at the start of a celebration of the Giants Super Bowl win over the New England Patriots at MetLife Stadium. At left is the Giants Justin Tuck. PHOTO BY TONY KURDZUK

ABOVE RIGHT: Giants fans try to reach and touch the Vince Lombardi Trophy as Brandon Jacons carries it around the perimeter of the stadium at the end of a celebration of the Giants Super Bowl win. PHOTO BY TONY KURDZUK

BELOW RIGHT: Cheering Giants fans fill the stands near a scoreboard showing the final score of the Giants Super Bowl win over the Patriots during a celebration of the victory at MetLife Stadium. PHOTO BY TONY KURDZUK

OPPOSITE: As confetti showers down Giants defensive end Justin Tuck hugs his 2-year-old son Jayce at the end of a celebration of the Super Bowl win. Tuck had the crowd of fans wish his son a happy birthday. PHOTO BY TONY KURDZUK

BY THE NUMBERS

Regular-Season Statistics

Passing

NAME	ATT	COMP	PCT	YDS	AVG	YDS/G	LONG	TD	TD%	INT	INT%	SACK	YDSL	RATE
Eli Manning	589	359	61.0	4933	8.4	295.9	99	29	4.9	16	2.7	28	199	92.9
Totals	589	359	61.0	4933	8.4	295.9	99	29	4.9	16	2.7	28	199	92.9

Rushing

NAME	ATT	YDS	AVG	LONG	20+	TD	YDS/G	FUM	FUML	1DN
Ahmad Bradshaw	171	659	3.9	37	3	9	54.9	0	0	42
Brandon Jacobs	152	571	3.8	28	1	7	40.8	3	0	32
D.J. Ware	46	163	3.5	17	0	0	10.2	0	0	7
Da'Rel Scott	5	16	3.2	8	0	0	1.5	1	1	1
Eli Manning	35	15	0.4	12	0	1	0.9	2	0	2
Victor Cruz	1	3	3.0	3	0	0	0.2	0	0	0
Steve Weatherford	1	0	0.0	0	0	0	0.0	0	0	0
Totals	411	1427	3.5	37	4	17	89.2	6	1	84

Receiving

NAME	REC	TAR	YDS	AVG	TD	LONG	20+	YDS/G	FUM	FUML	YAC	1DN
Victor Cruz	82	131	1536	18.7	9	99	25	96.0	1	1	595	59
Hakeem Nicks	76	133	1192	15.7	7	68	17	79.5	0	0	362	54
Jake Ballard	38	60	604	15.9	4	41	13	43.1	0	0	191	31
Mario Manningham	39	77	523	13.4	4	47	4	43.6	0	0	102	25
Ahmad Bradshaw	34	44	267	7.9	2	26	2	22.3	1	1	306	10
D.J. Ware	27	37	170	6.3	0	22	1	10.6	0	0	188	6
Bear Pascoe	12	16	136	11.3	0	22	1	8.5	0	0	93	7
Brandon Jacobs	15	23	128	8.5	1	40	1	9.1	0	0	120	6
Ramses Barden	9	19	94	10.4	0	26	1	11.8	0	0	23	5
Travis Beckum	5	10	93	18.6	1	67	1	7.2	0	0	40	2
Henry Hynoski	12	16	83	6.9	0	14	0	7.5	0	0	83	6
Domenik Hixon	4	6	50	12.5	1	22	1	25.0	0	0	6	3
Devin Thomas	3	3	37	12.3	0	14	0	2.3	0	0	14	2
Da'Rel Scott	2	2	13	6.5	0	9	0	1.2	0	0	5	0
Brandon Stokley	1	3	7	7.0	0	7	0	3.5	0	0	4	0
Totals	359	589	4933	13.7	29	99	67	308.3	2	2	2132	216

Defense

NAME	SOLO	AST	TOT	SACK	YDSL	TLOSS	PD	INT	YDS	LONG	TD	FF	REC	TD	BK
Antrel Rolle	82	14	96	0	0	2	4	2	-1	0	0	1	0	0	0
Michael Boley	74	19	93	1	6	4	3	0	0	0	0	1	3	1	0
Jason Pierre-Paul	65	21	86	16.5	112	8	6	0	0	0	0	2	0	0	1
Mathias Kiwanuka	62	22	84	3.5	28	12	2	1	9	9	0	1	1	0	0
Kenny Phillips	59	23	82	0	0	1	11	4	50	31	0	1	0	0	0
Jacquian Williams	58	20	78	1	8	1	4	0	0	0	0	0	3	0	0
Deon Grant	45	19	64	1	10	1	6	1	0	0	0	1	0	0	0
Aaron Ross	46	14	60	0	0	1	12	4	19	19	0	0	0	0	0
Corey Webster	43	8	51	0	0	1	16	6	71	25	0	0	0	0	0
Linval Joseph	34	15	49	2	15	2	4	0	0	0	0	0	0	0	0
Chris Canty	31	16	47	4	20	6	1	0	0	0	0	0	0	0	0
Justin Tuck	26	11	37	5	40	2	3	0	0	0	0	1	0	0	0
Greg Jones	26	5	31	0	0	1	0	0	0	0	0	0	0	0	0
Rocky Bernard	15	15	30	0	0	0	0	0	0	0	0	1	1	0	0
Chase Blackburn	20	6	26	0	0	1	2	1	9	9	0	0	0	0	0
Osi Umenyiora	16	9	25	9	64	1	1	0	0	0	0	2	0	0	0
Dave Tollefson	13	8	21	5	32	0	1	0	0	0	0	2	1	0	0
Tyler Sash	12	5	17	0	0	0	0	0	0	0	0	2	0	0	0
Prince Amukamara	12	2	14	0	0	0	3	1	0	0	0	0	0	0	0
Derrick Martin	8	4	12	0	0	0	0	0	0	0	0	0	0	0	0
Mark Herzlich	8	4	12	0	0	0	0	0	0	0	0	0	0	0	0
Spencer Paysinger	11	1	12	0	0	0	0	0	0	0	0	1	0	0	0
Zak DeOssie	8	2	10	0	0	0	0	0	0	0	0	0	0	0	0
Michael Coe	9	1	10	0	0	1	1	0	0	0	0	0	0	0	0
Will Blackmon	5	1	6	0	0	0	0	0	0	0	0	0	0	0	0
Devin Thomas	4	1	5	0	0	0	0	0	0	0	0	2	0	0	0
Jimmy Kennedy	2	2	4	0	0	1	0	0	0	0	0	0	0	0	0
Steve Weatherford	4	0	4	0	0	0	0	0	0	0	0	0	0	0	0
Ahmad Bradshaw	4	0	4	0	0	0	0	0	0	0	0	0	0	0	0
Justin Tryon	3	0	3	0	0	0	1	0	0	0	0	0	0	0	0
Chris Snee	2	0	2	0	0	0	0	0	0	0	0	0	0	0	0
Travis Beckum	1	1	2	0	0	0	0	0	0	0	0	0	0	0	0
Hakeem Nicks	2	0	2	0	0	0	0	0	0	0	0	0	0	0	0
Jake Ballard	2	0	2	0	0	0	0	0	0	0	0	0	0	0	0
Victor Cruz	2	0	2	0	0	0	0	0	0	0	0	0	0	0	0
Kareem McKenzie	1	0	1	0	0	0	0	0	0	0	0	0	0	0	0
Lawrence Tynes	1	0	1	0	0	0	0	0	0	0	0	0	0	0	0
Brian Williams	1	0	1	0	0	0	0	0	0	0	0	0	0	0	0
David Diehl	1	0	1	0	0	0	0	0	0	0	0	0	0	0	0
Michael Clayton	1	0	1	0	0	0	0	0	0	0	0	0	0	0	0
Brandon Jacobs	1	0	1	0	0	0	0	0	0	0	0	0	0	0	0
Will Beatty	1	0	1	0	0	0	0	0	0	0	0	0	0	0	0
Justin Trattou	0	1	1	0	0	0	0	0	0	0	0	0	0	0	0
Totals	861	270	1131	48	335	50	82	20	157	31	0	16	11	1	1

ACKNOWLEDGMENTS

BLUE HEAVEN CELEBRATES THE GIANTS 2011-12 season from their fast start to their midseason slump to a wild season ending run to the Super Bowl and the celebrations that followed.

This is the second Giants championship book *The Star-Ledger* has published. *One Giant Leap* came out after the 2007-08 season.

A project like this, under very tight deadlines, is an ambitious task. Managing Editor **Seth Siditsky** and Sports Editor **Drew van Esselstyn** edited the book. They combed through all the thousands of photos and words produced by the newspaper staff, coordinated with the publishing house and checked the many proofs to produce, what we think is, the definitive book on the season.

Giants beat writer **Mike Garafolo** truly is one of the best and his coverage of the team throughout the season was essential. From breaking news to thought provoking pieces, his coverage of the team is second to none.

Columnists **Steve Politi** and **Dave D'Alessandro** brought their own humor and analysis to the coverage, helping to give a broader perspective to the coverage. **Jerry Izenberg** once again wrote the forward to our Giants book as he continued his streak of covering every Super Bowl.

A book produced on deadline is ambitious to say the least and it wouldn't have been possible without the copying editing skills of **Brian Bailey, Patricia Cole, Brittney Davies, Steve Liebman, Moss Klein, Lauren Moore** and **Jennifer Potash.**

A big thanks goes out to **Chris, Nicole, and Brad Fenison.** They're the team at Pediment Publishing that keeps us on track (which we need) and always have a "can-do" attitude.

Bob Provost and **Doug Hutton** from the marketing department for their belief and support in making the book happen.

Jay Petrie in the advertising department for his efforts making sure everyone knows about this book.

Adya Beasley and **Rich Onyschak** for running digital cards and equipment for the Super Bowl.

And of course where would be without the photographers on the sidelines who showed us all of the plays and emotions from the season **Jennifer Brown, Aristide Economopoulos, Tim Farrell, Chris Faytok, Tony Kurdzuk, Andrew Mills, John Munson, John O'Boyle** and **William Perlman.** Without them there would not have been a book.